A Doctor's Story of LIFE and DEATH

Dr. Kakarla Subbarao

with

Arun K. tiwari

Ocean Books

Ocean Paperbacks

A Division of Ocean Books Pvt. Ltd.

ISO 9001:2008 Publishers

Published by
Ocean Paperbacks
A Division of Ocean Books Pvt. Ltd.
4/19 Asaf Ali Road,
New Delhi-110 002 (INDIA)
e-mail: info@oceanbooks.in

ISBN 978-81-8430-180-9
A Doctor's Story of Life and Death
by Dr. Kakarla Subbarao/ Arun K. Tiwari

Edition
First 2000; *Reprints* 2010 & 2013

Price
Rs. 150.00 (Rs. One Hundred Fifty only)

Printed at
Bhanu Printers, Delhi

Preface to the Second Decade Reprint

A decade has elapsed since the first publication of this book. It was reprinted in 2010 and remains in demand. My publishers suggested that I must write a Preface for the third reprint and share my story of the last ten years. It is indeed a satisfying feeling that my book was liked by the readers and has been accepted as part of curriculum in Medical Humanities course by the Hyderabad University. Every life is a story and there are many themes, plots and sub-plots that keep repeating. At 87, I am traversing through the last leg of my journey. Several friends and colleagues have departed and several others have receded into seclusion. I find myself fortunate to be active as a Radiologist and teacher of medicine. The Institutions that I helped created are functioning well and the International School run by my son and daughter-in-law has earned the reputation of one amongst the best and open for everyone irrespective to their financial status.

The privatisation and industrialisation of healthcare started in early 80's in India is complete. The healthcare industry is growing gloriously but as a commercial enterprise. Everything is available within the country and patients are coming from other countries to receive treatment in Indian hospitals. The healthcare is increasingly delivered in packages and through smart insurance deals. Doctors hop across hospitals for better engagement fee and diagnostics have become a highly networked enterprise. Medical Institutions are ranked according to the capitation fee they demand and get and sub-specialities are graded as per the price tag of their PG seat. When I opted to be a Radiologist in 1951 it was more to escape competition in surgery and general medicine. Today admission to Radiology PG seat goes for more than 10 million rupees.

I worked in American medical system for many decades and saw its gradual commercialization to the extent that half of Americans can't afford it any more. I have watched with interest the brave battle of President Barrack Obama to bring healthcare to every American and how what he started as a crusade ended with a compromise deal. Nevertheless the debate brought out a great awareness amongst the American people. The executives eating fried chicken and Fries with wine, beer and soda drinks are now switching over to Subway full grain breads with fresh vegetables over lemon tea and exercise sessions at the work place. Almost all food articles are fortified with nutrition.

Historically, the American Healthcare system evolved around life style diseases. There was always pure drinking water, sanitation and nutritious food for every one. In India we are yet to get these basic things and infections and water borne diseases continue to be rampant. Besides, there is a surge of indulgence with every extra thousand that are added to household income. More and more young professionals are turning in to habitual drinkers. You can find junk food outlets at every street and obese school children in every good school. First prolonged television viewing and now Internet surfing have taken away most of sports activities out of children daily schedules.

Indian pharmaceutical industry has done very well and made it mark at the global level. Best generic drugs are manufactured in India. However we have serious problems on the distribution side. There are spurious drugs in wide circulation. No user information is supplied with the drugs detailing contraindications and precautionary advice and doctors habitually write multi-drug prescriptions based on brand solicitation. In transfusion medicine, there are technologies like nucleic acid test (NAT), viral inactivation, and few techniques in immunohematolgy. Patients are mercilessly exploited under well-constructed monopoly. Corporate members have voting right in academic societies and almost all of them are controlled by business interests.

Ethics in the medical practice have been generalized to other sectors and all strands of the corruptions can be found in the medical practice. The biggest loser has been the medical education. A powerful group secretly influenced the matters of recognizing medical colleges. Across the country, Governments allowed self-financed medical colleges in the name of increasing the number of doctors for our growing population. A majority of these colleges take obnoxious sums of money to give admission to aspiring doctors. Governments have diverted healthcare budgets meant for district and Taluk level hospitals and primary healthcare centres to city based super speciality hospitals run by private companies.

Of course there is a silver lining. Increasing number of girls are taking medicine and nursing. Youth are well aware about perils of consuming tobacco and there is a trend towards regular exercise and healthy food. I wish we understand better the WHO definition of health which says, "Health is a state of complete physical, mental and social well-being and not merely the absence of disease or infirmity." Let there be more emphasis on mental and social well-being which is possible only through self-awareness. Through this Preface I put on record the importance of living a simple and uncomplicated life. You can't take away anything beyond this life. You can not even transfer it to your children without exposing them to fatal side-affects of un-earned money.

Let I be remembered as a teacher who returned to his students all that he learnt from his teachers, books and experience. There are flower pots in the International School I built on my ancestral property. I filled some of them with soil I brought from Pedamuttevi village in Krishna District where I was born. When the flowers blossom in these pots I can see my mother Manikamma and sister-in-law Lalitha. My village never went away from me.

—Kakarla Subbarao

Hyderabad
October 2012

O vanity of sickness! fierce extremes
In their continuance will not feel themselves.
Death, having prey'd upon the outward parts,
Leaves them invisible, and his siege is now
Against the mind, the which he pricks and wounds
With many legions of strange fantasies,
Which, in their throng and press to that last hold,
Confound themselves.

William Shakespeare
The Life and Death of Kind John
Act 5, Scene 7

Preface

I first saw Prof. Kakarla Subbarao while lying in the general ward of Nizam's Institute of Medical Sciences as a 32 year young scientist brought in from the Defence Research & Development Laboratory (DRDL) the previous night with heart racing towards death at 240 beats per minute. I was shifted there from ICCU after a life-saving defibrillation and night-long care. Neither the diagnosis written on my case sheet—Paroxysmal Supra Ventricular Tachycardia nor the tall sagacious Director making the rounds meant anything. As destiny had it, I survived the mishap to grow beyond missiles to medical technology landing in the Cardiovascular Technology Institute and taking to creative science writing.

For me the last 14 years had been full of growth and movement, turns and upheavals. Thanks to the treatment and care I received from my cardiologist, and now leader, Dr. B. Soma Raju I bounced back to work. The association between us later paved way for the historic initiative of my mentor Dr. APJ Abdul Kalam to open the doors of Defence Laboratories for the development of affordable medical devices as a spin-off of indigenous technology. During a very creative spell when many defence scientists worked with doctors everyone received support, guidance and inspiration from Prof. Kakarla Subbarao. While presenting him the first copy of *Wings of Fire,* I wrote with Dr. Abdul Kalam, I requested Prof. Kakarla Subbarao to grant me the opportunity to write his biography. He initially declined but later agreed on the condition that the biography would be addressed to patients and focus on the story of a doctor rather than his own personal story. I tried my best on both accounts and ended up with *A Doctor's Story of Life and Death,* the first book of its kind ever written in India.

This book bares open the secrets always discussed in medical circles in complex Latin and Greek words passed off as English to outsiders. It tells with an unprecedented honesty and transparency the limitations of modern healthcare system as well as science. But more than this, the book gives a rare confidence and support to the faceless patient who lives a double jeopardy of pain and financial hardship.

I always admired the matchless spellbinder in writer Irwing Stone who packed three great lives of all times into three excellent books: *Lust For Life* on painter Vincent Van Gogh, The *Agony and the Ecstasy* on the incredible genius of Michelangelo, and *The Passions of the Mind* on the father of modern psychology Sigmund Freud. The three books are as different in their style as the three persons they depict and their different professions. When I started writing with Prof. Kakarla Subbarao the first thing that amazed me was his surgical way of expressing thoughts. His expression was devoid of all emotional frills. He was blunt, fearless and brutally factual in whatever he narrated from his inner most feelings to his interpretation of scientific facts. Simultaneously he was very caring, courteous and grateful to people even in his memories. His views on health and healing—firmly rooted in science but drawing support from spirituality—are both indigenous and path-breaking.

The book lifts the phenomena of disease and death from the ordinary level of drugs and radiation and surgeries to the sublime of human existence and the bliss of life. The book not only activates the healing process deep within the body but also stretches the spiritual dimensions of the mind. There is a definite golden thread of divinity running through both the *Wings of Fire* and *A Doctor's Story of Life and Death.* At my personal level, if writing *Wings of Fire* was a pilgrimage, working on *A Doctor's Story of Life and Death* was attaining *Nirvana.*

It is my sincere hope that this book will inspire you, soothe you, lift your spirits and even trigger that inner source of healing and health that somehow get stifled and stuck amid the blitzkrieg of aggressive medication and commercially driven technological intervention. Getting these many fascinating facets of Prof. Kakarla Subbarao's outstanding persona, his wisdom and the most recent medical knowledge and prospects together in this book has done that for me, and I trust that reading it will do the same for you.

Prof. Kakarla Subbarao made me understand out of my own experience that within the symbolic experience of disease lies a path to change and self-healing and a healthy body mind. He made me start on that path. With the wisdom he bestowed upon me, I allowed my disease to heal my life. Let this book become a part of you and give you courage, confidence, and the power to live more victoriously and more purposefully.

I dedicate this book to my father Krishna Chandra Tiwari who lived the uneventful life of a lower-middle class bread-winner of a family of seven and died under ten days of intensive care in an ICCU. A disciplined life of 50 years and total abstinence from non-vegetarian food, alcohol and smoking could not prevent his coronary arteries from narrowing and chunks of his heart muscle from blood starvation. Finally the end came when a blood clot made the obstruction complete and choked off the already-compromised flow. The acutely starved heart muscles generating erythmatic electric impulses went into the chaotic squirming of ventricular fibrillation before settling for a final halt. My father, however, still lives in each of my 60 trillion cells that follow the code encrypted on the 23 chromosomes I inherited from him.

Arun K. Tiwari

Introduction

India is a land of Gods, Avatars and Gurus. More than one billion people live in this vast land of diverse geographic regions and long history. Most of them are believers. But more than allegiants of an almighty supreme power, they fear God as unknown. Everything that is unexplainable is seen as an act of God, every problem that is insurmountable is passed on to God for solution, every wish that is unachievable is presented before God for fulfilment. Most of the buck is passed on to God. Success is enjoyed in His name, failures are attributed to His indifference. There is an almost fatal fascination for the *status quo*. An inherent inertia can be seen in every walk of life. A lack of drive to come out of the rut is the most common trait among Indians. God has been idolised in hundreds and thousands of forms and is seen as an ombudsman out to bail one out of one's life problems including those related to health. Everything, everyone, has been segregated into the two compartments of good and bad, black and white, zeros and heroes. Everything is either sacred or sinful.

I am a physician by profession. More than five decades of working in hospitals has brought me very close to pain, suffering, and death. Looking around in my domain of healthcare I see more of pain than care. Problems outnumber solutions. There are crises related not only to individual and community health but also in the deliverance of healthcare. Unlike in Western countries, where medicine is practised as a *law monitored, insurance-driven* service profession, in India it is a very complex proposition involving handling of human emotions. Disease and pain are seen here as a punishment from God. Patients look at treatment as an exercise in atonement and salvation and approach doctors as they would, a priest in a temple—carrying all they have with folded hands and leaving egos outside as shoes. During the course of treatment, they fluctuate between helplessness and idle serenity and turbulence of restlessness and unsettling anxiety. Doctors often find themselves tangled in the web of these emotional loose ends and their own personal priorities for affluent life. This is a very peculiar situation that needs closer observation and careful analysis.

Sometime back I felt a strong desire to undertake such a study and write down my observations for further examination before they vanish into oblivion with my physical being. I felt that at the least my memories would provide an insight into the pain that a physician undergoes in his chosen profession of combating others' pain. I am no great achiever. There is nothing spectacular that has happened in my life and I certainly do not consider myself belonging to the category of people who write about their lives or are written about. Nevertheless, when I decided to write my memories, I could not go much farther than the pain and problems of my patients.

Lesser mortals always imitate legends. I took the clue from the great Mahatma Gandhi, who chose to write about his experiments with truth in his autobiography. I have decided to share with my readers about perhaps the only thing that I know—my experiences with my patients—why we suffer with so many sicknesses and what is it like to die. For doing this I needed someone who can hear me with the mind of a scientist and write it in a form that a reader relishes. I had teamed up with *Bharat Ratna* APJ Abdul Kalam in some of his Societal Missions concerned with making healthcare technologically enriched, affordable and accessible. This interaction had brought me closer to Arun K. Tiwari, his disciple and an outstanding scientist in his own right. The team of Dr. Abdul Kalam and Arun K. Tiwari had already produced the widely acclaimed masterpiece, *Wings of Fire*. It was, therefore, very natural that Arun and I teamed up to write the book you are about to read.

Why should anybody read my story? With a monotonous regularity my life revolved around the problems of my patients.

All I saw was suffering and people fighting pain. My patients were my all-consuming interest all along. I was talking to them all my years. I was listening to them all my days. Each patient was a book. Each patient was a teacher. Each patient was a personality—an integrated being having mental, emotional, social and physical characteristics. Each one brought to me a unique set of thoughts, fears, hopes, reactions, behaviours, and dreams, wrapped up in the form of diseases. Though suffering from widely known diseases, the problems of no two patients can ever be the same. Just as the physical body has a seemingly unlimited variety, so does the sickness that makes the body suffer. The response of the body to the disease is what makes each patient unique.

The latest research in genetics, molecular biology and neuroscience shows that many core physiological traits are inherited at birth, and that many of the differences between individual responses to disease are the result of differences in genes. Each one of us is created from the genes of our two parents. Each one of us is a product of generations of evolution, countless bits of information collected over millions of years, focused, narrowed, and refined until one is pushed out of the birth canal into the world. However, in spite of this inborn biological dimension, no one is really stuck up. There is an amazing built-in flexibility in each one of us that allows us to adapt to life's hurdles and challenges. Growing up means not only learning the ways of the world, but also dealing with one self. There is a body and there is a mind and both disease and healing hover between them.

Everyone has the ability to grow and change at every stage in life. People learn from experience, from parents and from friends. Individuals have the option to give in to temperamental weaknesses, or to overcome them. They can take advantage of temperamental gifts or hide them. People can indulge their desires to smoke, drink, or eat too much—or they can resist. They can live an active life or lock themselves in shackles of sedentary schedules and safe familiarity of habits. Sometimes they will do both during the course of their lives. The environment too plays a part but not as much as is popularly believed. The most important environmental factors are not reading, education, or social status, they are rather random and uncontrollable experiences such as precise concentration of a particular chemical in the brain, or something apparently minor like a childhood case of the measles. While we like to imagine ourselves to be the carefully crafted products of our upbringing and education, we are actually shaped by the same sort of chaotic events that make each *laddu* distributed at the Tirupati Balaji temple unique.

Just as a *laddu* has little to say about its shape, we are born with limits on the shape of our bodies, the colour of our skins and type of hair. Try as we might to change our shape, most of us will fail. We will eat the way we've always eaten, and we'll have the same activity level we had as children, or even earlier in the womb. There is an obese gene we all inherit that determines our body weight rather than the quantum of food we eat. Genes also control how quickly the body breaks down with age. A similar role is played by the genetics of gender—the biological differences between men and women. Every foetus is created without sex until a single gene switches on and begins a cascade of chemical reactions that turns half of us into males and half into females. The changes affect not only physical characteristics but also mental ones. Men are programmed to seek more partners and sexual novelty; women are serial monogamists seeking mates who will remain long enough to raise offspring.

Behaviour like addiction to alcohol, tobacco and dangerous drugs too is determined largely by heredity. It doesn't matter what substance you abuse if you are programmed to get hooked. People are driven to violence by a force within them in the form of certain brain chemicals. Each child shares personality traits with his or her parents, from talents to predisposition, to certain dreaded diseases. Every grown up man has experienced a shock of realisation when he does something exactly like his father before him. Every mother has a similar experience when a child behaves exactly like her. This is not bad; it's beautiful. This does not mean we are doomed to become our parents; it means we begin our journeys where our parents left off.

The book has been conceived with no other plan in mind than that of conversing with people who want to know more about pain and suffering related with the health of their loved ones as well as their own well-being. The text is organised into ten chapters and arranged in three parts—Cognition, Creation and Contemplation. The first part covers my childhood, medical education and initial years in the United States. The second part covers my comeback, retreat, growth and final return. The third part over-views the new emerging medical science based on molecular biology and genetics and records my views on going back to the basics of good living.

I have written this book as much for myself as for everyone who reads it. By writing about health and life, diseases and death I hope to recall the things I have seen and make them familiar to everyone else. If diseases may become just a bit more familiar to you, sickness will be less startling. To me, the view that sees physical disease in isolation from the soul is a blinkered one. Unless negative characteristics such as untruthfulness, malice, concealed aggression, a repressed urge to dominate others, unfocused intellectual energy, suppressed vitality and selfishness are diagnosed and treated, we will remain as condemned prisoners of medical contingency.

The entrance to divinity is through a pretty narrow door. If we want to pass through it, we must discard everything that sustains us in ordinary lives—everything that props us up and makes us feel safe, everything we know, trust, and rely on. In the healthy world of existence, if anything is fixed, it must be overthrown. If we lay claim to anything, that claim is rejected. If we cling to anything, it is torn from us. If we are proud of anything, it is held up to ridicule. Our illusions about ourselves are stripped bare. When we think we know something, it is made to be seen absurd. There are always many flaws lying peacefully inside our marvellous bodies capable of upsetting the entire delicately balanced equillibrium that is harmonious health. When and how these flaws trigger bouts of illnesses are all Life's ways of pulling from underneath our feet the rug that prevents us from making contact with the true ground of existence.

Like the stillness of death, in which all movement ceases, there is the stillness of Life in which nothing is left to check the movement of change. A stable system is not a system that never changes. It is a system that constantly and instantly adjusts itself and readjusts in order to maintain such a state of being that all sub-systems operate at maximal efficiency. Stability demands change to compensate for changing circumstances. Life is in fact inimical to permanence. Life is a constant surprise. Life's healthy mode is transition. Life manifests itself in only a never-ending process of dying and becoming. It is a strange fact of human experience that great suffering generates its own remedy. Let's evoke the Life's force by understanding the scriptures transcribed in our genes. If there are imperfections coded so are compensatory powers. The art and science of modern medicine can intervene to deal with the results of nature's imperfections, and to make use of nature's compensatory powers. The story I am going to narrate is that of the triumph of the human body, and of the human spirit. While pain is inevitable, suffering is optional.

Kakarla Subbarao

Hyderabad
June 2001

PART I

Cognition

Karm'endriyãni samyamya ya ãste manasasmaran
Indriy'ãrthãn vimûdhãtmã mithy' ãcãrah sa ucyate.

A man who restrains his body's powers and functions,
but who sits, turning over his mind
The objects of sense, deludes himself.
His conduct is pointless.

Bhagavadgita
Chapter 3; Verse 6.

1

Family legend had it that when I was born to Venkat Ratnam, a landlord in Pedamuttevi village in Kistna District of Madras Presidency (now Krishna District in Andhra Pradesh), and his wife Manikamma, as their fourth child. They were expecting a girl after having had three sons and a lost infant daughter. While an inheritor to the land is very much sought by every landlord, every other son born in the family is looked upon as a divider of family land. My father, waiting outside the delivery room for his daughter, returned to fields after hearing my first cries without even seeing the face of the fourth divider of his land. It was the third day after the *Sankranti* in 1925. I was given a modern version of my grandfather's name, Subbanna—Subbarao.

As a physician which I later became, I learned that there are very powerful childhood factors that programme one's brain with helpful as well as inappropriate responses. While I narrate some of my childhood memories, I will be attempting to create an awareness in you about how our childhood experiences have the potential and potency of affecting our later life. If we know how our brains have been programmed to respond to each emotion, we can prepare specific strategies to counteract, if not correct, our negative behaviour and bad habits that invariably carry within them the seeds of diseases and destruction of our lives.

Every human being is essentially an emotional person having runaway feelings. The feelings which, I feel, play a very important part in deciding our behaviour pattern and thereby the way we shape our lives are guilt, shame, anger, fear, jealousy, envy, apathy and unbridled love. I am not including sadness and disappointments in the list which, I feel, play a more important part in later life than in childhood. All of us, as children, have a driving, incessant need to make sense of ourselves, those around us, and the world in general. We constantly mix incoming information with a few things we know at that stage. Then we try to organise the new mix in ways that create some order out of what could be confusion, to bring meaningful interpretation to what could be meaningless. These childhood interpretations can have extremely potent impact later on in life. They carry the potential for achieving lots of benefits—or causing all sorts of mischief. Because they are the prime carriers of new meaning into our lives, these bits of language produce more sudden joy and more instant misery than any other education of the later life.

My eldest brother, Kasi Viswanath, 17 years old then, was married to Lalithabayamma. My earliest memories go to my third year where I found the love of two mothers, Manikamma and Lalitha. They found me the cutest child ever born and brought me up as the illusionary daughter of my father. Their tender caring, warmth and inexhaustible fountain of love made me like a fragile pampered little girl. My fair complexion and sharp features further fuelled their longing for a dancing doll in their courtyard. Soon, other girls and young ladies in the neighbourhood joined in their fantasy and started involving me in their plays and merry making. They used to take me along while going for bath and would leave their jewellery on me while in the water. This made me grow like *Gopi Krishna.* However, I could never come anywhere near his sensuality or cast any particular spell on anybody, except perhaps on Sarojini, although a little younger than me but always competing with my two *mothers* in caring. I can only reflect now that I used to see all girls as whole persons—more than seduceable bodies that bring relief and a sense of accomplishment.

I was really a blessed child. My first five years were like an extension of some divine abode that is thought to interlude between different forms of life the eternal soul keeps dwelling in. From these days, the later two years still linger in my memory as some beautiful dream, filled with so much love and care. There was no school in the village. My father had organised a school in a big veranda of our house. When the time came for me to be initiated into education, all I was asked was to sit there that was indeed the school. Even this constraint appeared to me as a rude shock and unbearable punishment. The first day, I went there and returned after peeping in to tell waiting Lalitha my achievement. But before I could reach the security of her open arms, my eldest brother (Kasi Viswanath) spanked me and pushed me back into the *school*. That was the first and the last day that I gravitated away from learning.

There were 25 students in the *school*. The teacher, Kosuri Ranga Rao, a 21-year-young man, used to come from a place two miles away from our village. He tried thrice in vain to attain the decoration with a Secondary School Leaving Certificate (SSLC) and finally settled as the leading light in my father's *academy* of enlightenment. His own achievements notwithstanding, Ranga Rao used to be very severe in imparting education to children. This, coupled with the discipline of my father, made the school veranda in our house quite a bit of scary place for lesser mortals like me. There used to be only two holidays in a month—the full moon and the new moon days—and the children used to watch moon's changing size with expectations every night. On many such nights, I and Sarojini would see the image of moon in each other's eyes too. Holding her hand and watching clouds playing hide-and-seek with moon is perhaps the most cherished memory I carry with me even today.

Besides Kasi Viswanath, the other two brothers—Venkateswara Rao and Bhasker Rao—were also cast in my father's mould. Traversing his footprints, they earned appreciation by their toil and the help they rendered my father in the fields. The over-protection I received from the ladies in the house, compounded by the innocent caring of Sarojini, made me over-sensitive to realities of life. Very simple and common things would appear harsh and painful and hurt me. Once, I was having a dischange from the ear and was called ugly by someone. It was such a terrible blow to my pride and sensibilities that I almost collapsed emotionally. A deep sense of anger, sadness and repulsion towards the stupidity of the remark filled me full, leaving no place for even a little bit of common sense to ignore trivialities.

In scientific terms, embarrassment, inferiority, shyness and loneliness are all seen as the emotion called shame. You feel shame when your self-esteem and well-being are too dependent on other people's approval. On a philosophical plane, it is hiding ourselves or parts of ourselves. You can see people biting their tongues instead of contradicting an obviously stupid suggestion at meetings because they are frightened to be seen as argumentative or supposed to be as children. So many people waste their lives by developing false-self through constantly trying to be someone they are not in order to please others and sink unnoticeably into the background.

The root cause of shame is low self-esteem. The feeling is triggered by any experience which makes us believe that we, as people, are not measuring up to a *good enough* standard in the eyes of the world outside us. People can feel shameful about their basic genetic inheritance such as their nose, feet, skin colour, height or even gender. We can only feel shame as a result of someone else's judgment. There are sets of grades against which we keep measuring ourselves. These are given to us, mostly in early childhood and often subtly by others. I feel shame is a social glue that helps societies gel together. By reinforcing certain shared values, certain people who don't measure up to these values are quietly made to sit at the bottom of the social pile. In our village, a high value was put on adventure and arrogance, making people who prefer a calm, safe, uneventful life to feel ashamed of their cowardly existence. This feeling made them less likely to challenge their arrogant masters, however aggressively and unjustly these leaders wielded their personal power.

Shame is, therefore, both an uncomfortable emotion and a very frightening one, because it is so bound up with social isolation. Not only are we inclined to hide when we feel it, others reject us and ignore us when they recognise that we are someone who don't match up to the required standard. In Indian villages, this aspect of shame is consciously cultivated, by the people in power, as a way of ensuring obedience.

Many labourers, including women in their tattered clothes and with crying infants clinging to their sagging bosoms, would squat outside our big house for hours waiting for my father to come out and pay their wages. I used to feel very disturbed by their presence and many times dared to plead their case for payment. Every time my father would chuckle and drown himself in deep slumber. This apathy towards the poor and helpless used to fill me with an intense feeling of anger and helplessness.

Apathy is an emotion that grows very slowly. It can be insidiously working away for years in our subconscious before we, or anyone else, even notice its presence. During its build-up its bad traits have much more chance of becoming deeply ingrained into our general personality than some of the more quick-firing emotions. My father who felt that he could not be bothered at the moment became eventually an uncaring person. I used to care for the poor labourers waiting outside. The threat to their well-being posed by my father's indifference left me frustrated and irritated.

As a child I was strong-willed and positive in my tastes, but never made any big fuss in expressing them. I seldom threw a temper tantrum. Yet I always managed to communicate my negative reactions quite plainly. I used to sincerely believe in education imparted by Kosuri Ranga Rao in the form of archetypes and cliches like honesty, obedience, discipline and duty towards society and country. One day, a servant child stole one mango from a room in the house where not less than a ton of them were stored. I caught him red-handed and reported the matter to my father with the pride of having performed a righteous and responsible act. My father disappointed me by brushing aside the whole incident as insignificant and preaching that small actions of small people should be overlooked. That all people were equal and any theft, small or big, was immoral was the general refrain. A feeling germinated in me that I must draw my own line between the realistically right and the practically wrong.

I was growing in curiosity too. Every month Lalitha would be isolated in her room during her menstrual period. I never liked it. When I questioned my mother about the rationale, I was told that if she touched milk during those days it would turn into curd and, therefore, she had to be away from the kitchen. I remember dipping her finger forcefully in milk before drinking it and touching her to see if anything wrong could emanate from someone as nice and lovely as Lalitha.

The innocent and passive ideation of life where Gods and Demons participate in your daily chores and eventually are responsible for what good and bad you receive has never appealed to me. There was an ancient temple of Lakshmipathy Swamy (Lord Vishnu, the sustainer God in Hindu mythology married to the Goddess of wealth Lakshmi) in front of our house. In fact our village is known across miles for the temple. I used to regularly visit the temple and felt comfortable inside. The chanting of prayers and the aroma of incense sticks created a pleasantly mystic environment. Whenever some marriage was performed and the bride and the bridegroom were brought to the temple in a procession led by a group of village musicians playing Nadaswaram and some improvised percussion instrument, almost all children assemble there. Many such times Sarojini and I exchanged sly glances and experienced the thrill of stealing something precious away from the crowd.

One Swamiji used to live on the outskirts of our village. This place was known as Krishnashram. He gave discourses to the villagers on religious matters and offered counselling when they came confused or troubled. Swamiji was good in Sanskrit and Hindi. I started going there to learn Hindi from him. The thing that amazed me the most in Swamiji was his belief in himself. He was so sure about his powers that he would confidently touch the sick to ward away illness. He was said to have a divine vision and he could detect thieves and even locate hidden treasures. I personally never witnessed any such miracles nor believed in these claims beyond a point of general awe and surprise. One day while I was taking lessons in Hindi in Krishnashram, a big snake whizzed past me. I was gripped with fear. Our family took it as a most frightening incident and it took me more than a week to cajole my mother into allowing me to go to the Ashram again.

After finishing seven years of education under the watchful eye of Kosuri Ranga Rao, the question arose if I had to be sent away for further education. There was no such dilemma faced in case of my second brother Venkateswara Rao whom my father overheard saying to his friends that why was he (my father) not buying a cow instead of wasting 50 rupees on sending him (Venkateswara Rao) to school. There were second thoughts on sending me away because of the possessiveness my mother and Lalitha developed about me. I, though totally drowned in the warmth of their love and care, wanted to go away and study further. Does gender differentiation really exist in the form and substance of intangible feelings? One wants to hold and keep and the other wants to go away.

The nearest school was at Challapalli, eight miles south-west of Pedamuttevi towards River Krishna. I had to walk the entire distance. My father came about a mile to see me off. My third brother Bhasker Rao, himself a student of the same school at the SSLC level, accompanied me to Challapalli. My mother and I wept for quite sometime. Lalitha gave me a good quantity of *Pakodi* for eating on the way. I was put up in a hostel.

As if to prove myself different from others, I began to organise my life into a routine rather early. The early years of protected care and tender love grew into focused efforts and compassion. Notable among other students in the class was Visalakshi, sister of the Chieftain of Challapalli, Srimanthu Raja Yarlagadda Siva Ram Prasad. She used to draw lot of attention from teachers and other students. The whole set-up here was so different from that at Pedamuttevi. I knew quite early that I no more occupied the centre of attention and care. If anything what Visalakshi returned to me was a glance full of vanity and an invitation to compete.

In school I was obedient, studious and reliable but was reluctant to participate in class discussions. I used to refuse directives for recitations and elocutions from teachers and elders and was even called as timid, lacking confidence and self-centred. I utilised every possible opportunity to go home. A new sense of enlightenment started growing in me. Whenever I came to Pedamuttevi, I found myself a visiting observer, a detached analyst. I started disliking things about my village, it's people, it's ways of organising and destabilising things. The endless talking among people started bothering me. Years of idle lifestyle whetted the appetite of my village folks, mostly relatives, to advise others pathologically. I saw so much of it that I had come to consider the whole process as turning private woe into public comedy. I am of the belief that advice is seldom welcome, and those who need it most like it the least.

Meanwhile, Bhasker Rao completed his SSLC and returned to Pedamuttevi to be the son of the soil. My best efforts to be the first in the class would get negated by the stature of Visalakshi's brother which fetch her almost always a couple of additional marks. It could also be the illusion of my egoist self which always believed itself to be the best. But then that was how I felt at that point of time. There are profound moments, rare situations and times of extreme personal attachment in daily life when most people reflect automatically, immediately and intuitively. When we confront another's intense self-disclosures we are left speechless. We acknowledge that we have indeed registered the message. The visceral reaction of teachers always showed that they were on Visalakshi's side. They would reflexively say good things to me to confirm that my discomfort towards their happiness in helping Visalakshi had been taken in and taken seriously.

My performance level was so unknowingly becoming dependent on Visalakshi that my relationship with her was almost jeopardised. Jealousy is usually accompanied by anxiety, and often leads to anger, which is usually turned outwards rather than inwards. If the feelings are kept secret, shame usually grows and flourishes. It is frequently confused with envy, where you need something which you don't have. But although the two emotions have distinctly different triggers, they do ride in tandem because some of their root causes are common. Our urgent psychological hungers often cause us to swallow without tasting. The reveal-conceal ordeal is among the costliest conflicts of human relations. Most of the time, the solution simply lies in learning how and when to move towards the reveal side.

I found an inspiring guide in my Telugu teacher Suranna. He would read my unexpressed feelings and teach me to give words to them. I learned poetry from Suranna and wrote many verses, mostly addressed to Sarojini but never shared with her or with anybody else for that matter. I was the poet and I was the listener too. The writer and the reader both rolled into one. Later, communistic ideas started substituting love and longing in my writings. I wrote a poem for the school magazine depicting a car throwing exhaust on a beggar's face, in contempt.

One night in the hostel, while we were taking dinner, electricity failed. Amid confusion and chaos, everybody shouting at everybody else in pitched darkness, our cook-cum-server Lakshmaiah put his foot on my plantain leaf. This filled me with rage and I threw the leaf with the remains of food on Lakshmaiah's back. The whole place got frozen and was filled with tension. Immediately hostel warden Kasi Ramaiah appeared on the scene wielding his cane. He slapped me on my face. Blood gushed to my ears under the impact. For a moment, Lakshmaiah, Kasi Ramaiah and I were turned to a Bermuda Triangle ready to gobble up anything. Minutes got stretched into an eternity. Finally Kasi Ramaiah broke the silence and took me to his house putting his hand on my shoulder. His wife served me food and brought me back to ease. On return, I met Lakshmaiah and apologised. He himself had not eaten dinner and was waiting for me with the food.

Anger is always taught to be dangerous, something that would just get you into trouble. We are told that if we give in to anger we'll go crazy. I don't subscribe to these general attitudes about the feeling of anger. Though it is bad to burst into irritability or rage at the wrong time, in the wrong place and at wrong people or objects, suppressing tension and rendering ourselves speechless, motionless, depressed and sick is much worse. I hate crying victim's tears that always invite more abuse. I believe anger under control gives us more confidence to stand up for our own and other's rights.

Chandra Rajeshwar Rao was a popular young communist leader in Challapalli. He would go around with tremendous energy and charisma. I was almost fascinated by his talks and the way he met and intermingled with people, giving big words to their small problems. I started knowing more of politics of poverty and property. Those who had property exploited those who did not have. It was called communism and considered anti-establishment. Rajeshwar Rao's friends would give younger students posters written with *Long Live Revolution.* These posters would be pasted in public places at 3 in the morning to avoid police. I was so excited with the idea of doing something against the establishment that getting up so early filled me with a great sense of duty and satisfaction.

Though Rajeshwar Rao talked about Marx and Lenin and never mentioned Gandhi and Nehru, I used to read about them with reverence. To me both Gandhi and Marx were equally appealing. The dignity of labour, equal right to existence, simplicity, sacrificial quality to help others and social justice were sacred to me. I read *Kranti,* a Hindi translation of some Russian publication, with interest and found it very close to my own mind-set. The political environment was getting hotter. Gandhiji gave the Quit India call. It spread like a wildfire among students. I got myself so involved in all this that I fasted when Gandhiji fasted. I found fasting difficult but used to feel a vague sense of purification at the end of the fast. A strong feeling of nationalism gradually got seated in the depth of my mind and at times I felt almost compelled to quit studies and go to jail.

Around the same time, my father made a bad land deal. He bought a big stretch of land at a good price, overlooking its low elevation. During rains, the entire land got flooded and crops were washed away. I visited my village during harvest time and found not even two bags full of paddy from the entire crop. The financial loss coupled with injury to his pride for making a wrong decision was too much to bear for my father. Behind his arrogant and authoritarian tough outer shell I found him a simple and contended person. His personal possessions were limited to two pairs of cotton dress. While carrying two bags of paddy back home in our bullock cart, I heard a relative inquiring how many more ferries we planned to bring home for the bonanza. Rajeshwar Rao's talk of equal distribution of property and Gandhiji's on dignity of the fellow-being looked so misplaced against this uncoloured meanness and unsheathed jealousy.

Eighty per cent of the population in Pedamuttevi belonged to the *Kamma* caste. Almost everybody was related to everybody else. This means, a few generations back they were from one family. Being the youngest child I used to sleep in my parents' room and listen to them talking about all that was not good among the villagers. If we were all linked to a common heritage and lineage of some superior blood what was then the rationale behind this almost sadistic response? We talk so much about social equity, justice, religious tolerance—all big words. Why nobody talks about our emotional barrenness and toxic jealousy that can kill any compassion and kindness in any relationship? I read a good poem that was perhaps written for the likes of my people:

There are six things, which the God hates,
Seven which are an abomination to him:
Haughty eyes, a lying tongue,
And hands that shed innocent blood,
A heart that devises wicked plans.
Feet that make haste to run to evil,
A false witness who breathes out lies,
And a man who sows discord among brothers.

When I was giving my eighth standard examination, I acted as conduit, transferring a chit carrying answers from one student to another, in the examination hall. I was caught by the invigilator in this act of plain copying amounting to cheating. As I had no intention and even the necessity to derive any advantage out of the act, I felt miserable having been into it. The other two students were debarred from the examination but I was left with a stern warning in view of my brilliant academic record and evidence of innocence. However, this had left a scar on my psyche. Your surroundings, the people who live with, can really make you sick. You have a good chance of ending up as a loser if you live in the company of failures. My friends in the examination halls were opportunistic users. Then there were control freaks, meddlers, narcissists, instigators, emotional refrigerators, liars. These people had to be stopped in their tracks. How? Suddenly, lessons in life started looking tougher than the school syllabus. By the time, I finished my high school at Challapalli, I was emotionally toughened.

Out of all subjects, I excelled particularly in mathematics. This made my father proud, for a change. Circumstance had attenuated his arrogance to a great extent. I was welcomed back as a hero. The decision to send me on higher studies was spontaneous and unanimous. The only hitch was between me and Sarojini. She was of marriageable age by the standards of those times and if I went for further education, either I had to marry and leave her alone, or she would be married to someone else and I would be left alone.

I landed at Hindu College, Masulipatnam, which was considered the best. The port city of Masulipatnam, now called Machillipatnam, but always known as Bandar locally, was across the canal, bringing Krishna water to the fields. There were many big buildings in Masulipatnam built by Britishers as they arrived in this land from Madras by the sea route. The influence of British was evident. At the college, when they questioned me about how much I scored in English I reported them a grand 22% which was the highest at Challapalli that year. A frog leaped out of the well!

The Quit India movement was at its peak. My feelings of nationalism, stifled to an extent for family considerations, were roused. This, compounded by the hurt caused by Sarojini marrying someone else, made me think once again of leaving college and joining Satyagraha. However, the still disarrayed financial fortunes of my father and brothers at home and my own basic equation with education held me back. I, however, attended political meetings and rallies and took active interest in happenings there. One day agitators decided on setting the Masulipatnam Railway Station on fire. A big crowd of students gathered at the station. There were policemen, on horses, fiercely wielding batons. The entry to the station was blocked. Frustrated and unable to give vent to their anger, the students started stoning the policemen. I also lifted a stone and was about to hit a policeman when I saw blood oozing out of a wound on his forehead. What am I doing? What for? Whom are we hurting? A silent communication took place between that man riding a horse on someone's orders and a boy planning to hurl stones in a frenzy. The enlightenment of each other's helplessness about what was happening froze me. I dropped the stone and walked out of the crowd.

I heard about Sarojini's marriage, but had no guts to go and see her tying the nuptial knot to someone else. As someone has written, "There is nothing half so sweet in life as love's young dream." If what they say about eternal life cycles and soul taking different body forms were true, we had already met in the present forms and a union in the sense of husband and wife was to wait for some other life. A part of me had died at that tender age itself. It was a deep emotional wound, that too a self-inflicted one.

Can I afford to become soft and soppy about my emotional pain? Aren't most pleas of emotional distress just convenient excuses to evade responsibility? Why should I heal? Wouldn't a life of flat, colourless and stagnant happiness be worse—I may be hurting internally, but with my pain am I still alive? I used to sit on a see-saw of hope and despair, gloom and determination, vision and deception. I took sometime to realise that there are good reasons for healing emotional wounds promptly and efficiently.

If emotional pain is not managed, whatever be the cause and however old the hurt, we have less resistance to other hurts; we are likely to be more fearful of potentially good opportunities which could be emotionally strengthening; we can experience emotional confusion, caused by inappropriate feelings leaking into a current situation; we are in danger of losing control if a feeling from an unhealed wound is echoed and inappropriately amplified; we endanger our ability to feel and express positive emotions such as excitement and compassion. Though saddened and weary, I pulled myself together and went into my studies more as a solace than anything else in scholastic terms.

I passed my Intermediate examination with good marks. Although an uncle of mine wanted me to become a police officer and another one a village administrator, my zeal to become an engineer propelled me to go to Madras and explore the possibilities of getting admitted into an engineering college. I stayed there for a month pursuing the matter but some sort of quota by caste was introduced and that denied me an admission. Judging prospects of getting admission into engineering as bleak, as a backup strategy I obtained an application for a medical seat but never filled it up. I returned to Masulipatnam to join BA course in the same college. I was heart-broken as I would have to become some one in the crowd. One day I discovered the previous year's application form for the medical seat, carefully filled it and posted. I forgot about the whole thing as deep inside I was not keen on becoming a doctor. To my utter surprise, I received a postcard from an acquaintance, Nageswar Rao, in Madras. The postcard said that I had been allotted a Medical Seat at Visakhapatnam.

The next thing I did was to take my friend Padmanabhiah with me and reach Nidumolu. From there we took a bus to Bezwada (now Vijayawada) to board a train to Visakhapatnam. The postcard was factual: I was selected for admission in MBBS course in the Andhra Medical College, and all I had to do was to deposit Rs. 420 and confirm admission. It was big money and we could arrange the deposit by collecting small amounts from friends and acquaintances in Visakhapatnam. On way back, I went to Pedamuttevi and informed my family about my admission in the Medical College. The first reaction was one of dismay. There was a conference of all family members and relatives to discuss the acts of omission and commission of this belligerent youth. The fraternity finally endorsed what I had already done and I left the village the next day. As the great Chinese book *I Ching* says, "The superior man, when he stands alone, is unconcerned, and if he has to renounce the world, he is undaunted," I was indeed alone and in fact renounced my village.

□

2

There were about fifty students in the first year batch of MBBS at Andhra Medical College with me. Almost all of them were from Andhra region, representing both urban and rural areas. The difference in their backgrounds was very explicit in their daily lifestyles and mannerisms. While students from urban areas would take the formal wear of socks and boots to as far as the bathrooms and use English even in their most intimate conversations, students from rural background would carry contemptuous aggression for their urban colleagues and miss no opportunity to let them down. There was a strong underlying divide between the two groups which would manifest at any given opportunity of power play as trivial as election of the mess secretary or selection of the volleyball team. I could not identify myself with any of them and thus won the acceptance of both or perhaps was considered to be of no consequence. Five students were admitted in the quota created for refugees from Western Punjab. Many of my flagellant colleagues discovered some repelling body odour in them. I found none and became in fact quite friendly later with S.S. Bhalla, one among them.

During the familiarisation phase, Dr. Shepherd interviewed me. A British, Dr. Shepherd always had his personal secretary when he talked to *natives* to fill any possible gap that might arise between the ideas expressed in his Oxford-accented English and the mumbling of novices in their Telugu-tainted version of his great language. During my interview, the personal secretary, almost tanned in the reflected glory of his boss, whispered into my ears, 'Wish him". I said, "I don't fish", mistaking his advice for wishing

Dr. Shepherd to a query about fishing. I always wondered as a child about the relevance of priests during prayers. My confusion became further compounded.

I had interest in Mathematics and considered Biology as an unavoidable burden. In the first class of Biology, I was asked to lift an earthworm. I looked around for a fork, inviting laughter from my colleagues and a frown from my teacher. "How will you handle a dead body if the touch of an earthworm is frightening to you?" somebody said. More as a challenge than for the logic of the contemptuous comment, I lifted the earthworm and kept it on my palm. At night I kept feeling the creature's movement even after washing my hands a dozen times.

Slowly, I started enjoying observing different forms of living creatures. Within six months, I extended my circle of acquaintances from earthworms to rats, frogs and rabbits. While going for our lecture classes we passed through a corridor that housed the Museum of Anatomy. A part of the museum was used to perform autopsy. My curiosity used to lead me to the museum where I would observe corpses in silence. The cold and stillness of death would fill me with a strange kind of realism. The clever manipulations, pretensions, plots, pride, prejudices, greed, so familiar and almost omnipresent, would appear so strange and remote in the presence of the human corpse.

Most of our teachers in the Medical College were Tamil doctors. I developed instant fondness for my anatomy professor Dr. Krishna Rao. He was very tall, six feet four inches, and lanky. He would utter the fairly long and tongue-twisting medical terms describing human anatomy, mainly adopted into English from Greek and Latin, with such ease and fluency that students used to circle around him. Barring a turban, I used to see Sarvepally Radhakrishnan in him. Unfortunately, he left the college after about three months of my joining.

My tryst with medical English, however, continued. The features of human body visible to the naked eye make morphological anatomy, the hidden ones that need a microscope involve histology. The basic framework of the body is provided by a large number of bones that collectively form the skeleton.

The flexible tissue around them is cartilage. Two bones are united together by fibrous bands called ligaments. The flesh is muscles. On getting an electrical signal from brain they contract and thus provide power for movements. Running through the intervals between muscles are blood vessels, lymphatic vessels and nerves. Blood vessels are tubes through which blood circulates. The vessels that carry blood from the heart that keeps pumping it to maintain circulation, to various tissues are arteries, and the ones that return this blood to the heart are veins. Tissues, arteries and veins are connected by a fine network of microscopic vessels called capillaries. Lymphatic vessels are delicate, thin walled tubes, difficult to see. They run alongside veins and have bean-shaped nodes in between called lymph nodes. Running along with them are solid chord-like nerves that carry electric impulses from and to the brain.

In addition, there are specialised organs called viscera. Some of the viscera are solid like liver and kidney, some are tubular like intestines or sac like stomach. The viscera are grouped together in accordance with the function to form various organ systems. So, respiratory system provides body with oxygen, alimentary or digestive system absorbs food, urinary system removes waste and genital system contains organs concerned with reproduction.

A major problem in describing anatomical relationships is that they keep changing with movement. When a patient is standing, his head is his uppermost part and feet the lowermost. But when he is lying down, both head and feet are at the same level. So, we were taught to presume that patient is standing upright, looking directly forwards, arms held by the side of the body and palms facing forwards with thumbs lying outwards. Now, anything that is nearer to the front of the body is anterior, and anything behind it is posterior. Anything closer to the head is superior to anything below which is, thus, inferior. The vertical plane that divides body into right and left is median. Anything nearer to it is medial and away is lateral. So each eye is anterior to the corresponding ear and is also medial to it. A doctor would, therefore, say that the eye is anteromedial to the ear and that nose is inferomedial to the eye. It was learning a new language.

I shared room with Papa Rao, a native of Gudavalli, in the hostel. I found many things common between us. Papa Rao's basic truthfulness, compassion and an innocent frankness in expressing feelings made me feel comfortable in my otherwise forced compliance with the life at Visakhapatnam. Here, there was total absence of culture, refinement and dignity of living to which I almost got addicted to at Bandar. The sight of ladies wearing no blouses, having heavy rings hanging in their ear lobes and nose, almost disfiguring them, and smoking cheap cigars backwards (keeping burning end inside) were repulsive to me, at the least. There was only one road, about a mile long, in the name of civilization and the stench of fish all around would make me sick. The sound of bombs dropped by Japanese used to scare me. We used to hide ourselves under tables as a reflex action on hearing sirens warning of a possible air strike. Fortunately, nothing befell on me or around me.

The freedom movement was nearing its peak. It was almost certain that the British would go. My fascination with Student Congress was turning into an obsession and I was not able to concentrate on my studies. During this period, my family proposed that I should marry the granddaughter of one of my uncles. I found them too close and too familiar to be anything else. My mother was getting restless for being unable to settle her son in matrimony. Her fears ranged from my becoming a revolutionary to my marrying some city girl. Another proposal came from another relative, a friend of brother Bhasker Rao. The girl Lakshmi, lone child of Venkat Ramaiah and his wife Sriravama, five years younger than me, was proposed and I accepted her as my would be bride. We got married on May 13, 1945.

My maternal grandfather, Venkatramaiah, was a very quiet and withdrawn person. He used to obey my maternal grandmother, Sheshamma, with reverence and live under some selfless surrender in copybook obedience. When Lakshmi came to our house after marriage, she was wearing a lot of jewellery and looked as if she were coming out of some fairy tale cinema. My grandfather made a surprise comment, "Does the jewellery actually belong to her or on display as family wealth?" Lakshmi's cheeks turned red. My grandmother gave my grandfather her dirtiest look and hugged my wife away from the stupid remark. Interestingly, the boy considered earlier as alliance for Lakshmi by her parents got married to the girl proposed initially to me. This little bit of reshuffle eventually makes bloodlines and generations so unique and so different from each other. How many people actually realise the importance of this subtle fine-tuning on our lives and that of our offsprings?

On the 13th day of our marriage I had fever, which was later diagnosed as Typhoid. I was at Lakshmi's place and used to have severe headache and would be half asleep for over a week. As my mother-in-law was not supposed to see me or interact with me, and Lakshmi was too young to take care of me, my grandmother, mother and Lalitha would be at my bedside, supposedly on turns, but almost always present simultaneously. In the second week, I felt better and was given some food. Unfortunately, the infection relapsed and I was bed-ridden for another month. I could come out of the bed only after forty two days and immediately rushed to Visakhapatnam, leaving Lakshmi with her parents.

It was interesting to know, later in the college, that Typhoid is an infectious disease contracted by eating food or drinking water contaminated with the bacterium *salmonella typhi.* I was in fact appalled to learn that the infection comes from the faeces of a person who has the disease or who is a symptomless carrier of the causative bacteria. As nobody was known to be suffering from fever in the village, it emanated from some symptom-less carrier among those many who would defecate in the open each morning. Flies would carry the bacteria from the infected faeces to food. During the development of the disease, the bacteria pass from the intestines into the blood, and then to the spleen and liver, where they multiply. In colloquial terms Typhoid is, therefore, called the fever of the stomach. The village doctor would diagnose it by abdominal tenderness and constipation suddenly turning into diarrhoea. The enlargement of liver and spleen is also felt.

On the night of 14th August, 1947, we were all awake and excited to receive Independence. Nobody slept in our hostel. However, there being nothing specific to do everybody was talking to everybody else. All India Radio broadcast the midnight session of Parliament live. Our local Congress leader Tenneti Viswanatham hoisted the Indian Tricolour flag at the stroke of midnight—a historic moment, before which we were subjugated, and after which we turned sovereign. Was that all so simple, straightforward, smooth? For a moment, it looked too abstract, intangible, symbolic, intellectual, away from the realm of the ground realities of life. I got up the next morning to the same reality that was there the day before. At streets, the common people were not even talking about freedom. In fact they slept well that night and were having no hangover. Life was absolutely routine and unchanged for them. Semantics apart, did I feel any change?

For many years I found my mission in living in a free India. What does it really mean to live in a free country? What does constitute freedom for an individual? Are the people crowding the roads not free? Free to smoke, free to litter, free to reproduce irresponsibly, free to shun the light of reason and education and live under darkness of superstition, black magic and occult. Are people owning land not free? Free to use it as a tool to govern the lives of others rather than as a business asset and capital resource. Are people holding government positions not free? Free to derive personal profit from every public issue. In fact, I found no real evidence of some real extraneous source of injustice or exploitation, something bad that can be truly attributed to the British Rule. To me everything appeared perfectly intrinsic, like a bacterium taking over the entire organism. The departure of the British, however, created a void as far as the target of my aggression and restlessness was concerned. Instead of dwelling on such deeper and depressing questions, I thought it better to focus on my studies without any further delay or newer distraction.

Patients had become my new focus. While on rounds, I would turn back at anybody crying, forgetting other patients and the order in which to proceed. In fact, I used to be amazed by the expressionless faces of nurses and my senior doctors and their mechanical responses. My patients were very simple. They were like innocent children. An old lady, when I asked her age, told me, with rich gestures, to find out for myself as, in her opinion, a doctor should know everything. The hopes of innocent people would not be confined to the domain of the treatment they should get for a particular health problem. Landed up in the hospital and with nothing else to fill their time, they used to seek total solutions to their life problems with the active participation of their friends and relatives attending on them.

The examination techniques that doctors use include visual examination of the ears, eyes, nose, throat and skin. They listen to the chest through a stethoscope, feel body parts such as abdomen or armpit to detect tenderness or swelling, called palpation, test reflexes, and tap chest or abdomen with the fingers to see from the vibrations whether the different internal organs appear to be normal, called percussion. The doctor may take temperature to see whether patients have fever, measure blood pressure, take pulse, or weigh them. In case of females, pelvic examination is also done and vagina is examined visually and manually to see if the reproductive organs seem to be healthy and our cultural outlook in this matter created a very indigenous clan of *lady doctors*.

I had developed a knack for giving injections. I would engage the patient in a conversation to minimise his anxiety and allay his exaggerated fear about being pricked with the needle and then give him the injection in an instant. Sometimes I feel that the doctor-patient relationship boils down to getting and giving attention. Failure of a patient to get the attention of the doctor is a major and sometimes tragically underestimated phenomenon that figures in his or her recovery. Is not it attention-grabbing that makes infants cry, children whine, wives fume, husbands pout, bosses fret, employees complain, and teachers nag? Attention does much to determine our sense of self-worth. We value it more than we like to admit. Attention is such a precious commodity that people attempt suicide for it. People have killed because they are attention-denied for too long.

The common diseases were fevers. As there was no diagnostic laboratory or X-ray around, I would look for accompanying symptoms. If the patient is short of breath even when resting and coughing brownish sputum chest infection such as pneumonia would be a possibility. Severe headaches, stiff neck, vomiting, drowsiness and confusion would announce inflammation of membranes around the brain, called meningitis. But if limbs are aching with a running nose or sore throat it would be influenza. Clear cases of sore throat would be pharangitis or tonsilitis. Pain in side of the back with pink or cloudy urine or pain while passing urine would be an acute infection in kidney such as cystitis, glomerulonephritis, or pyelonephritis. With chills it would be malaria, with nausea typhoid.

Many patients would come with tuberculosis, called TB. We would recognise it with coughing involving blood-stained sputum, chest pain, shortness of breath, fever, sweating at night, poor appetite and weight loss. A majority of patients would come very late having either fluid or air collected between lungs and chest wall. In case of fluid we would call it as pleural effusion, and in case of air, pneumothorax. There would be many cases daily with dysentery. Also, many patients would come with leishmaniasis, called Kala-azar.

Drugs were given absolutely free in the hospital. They were not many however. Antibiotics had not arrived and sulfa drugs were the ultimate panacea. In addition to free drugs, the patients would be given one boiled egg as a nutritional add-on. I saw many patients hiding their egg under their pillows and selling it for buying cigars. If caught they would give a shameless grin exposing their tobacco-tainted teeth. A wave of anger at their meanness and my helplessness in changing them would run through me.

We had one more Subbarao in our batch. He would always wear a jovial and smiling face—a cute and nice image of a doctor as a friend to the patient. A real private practitioner in the making. Patients would identify him as Dr. Smiling Subbarao leaving my identity as Dr. Serious Subbarao. I always detested artificial mannerisms and facemasks to suit occasions and fit situations. To me dealing with integrity was what mattered most. The emphasis on the response I should evoke in the person with whom I was dealing had never caught my attention. Most of my student colleagues would dance around Professors and sing praising carols. I almost failed in this art to the extent that I found myself incompetent in even attempting that. A silent good morning was what I offered to my teachers and a kind delivery of knowledge was what I sought from them. After more than fifty years since then I can say that all of them were not kind and I was not an ideal student.

During my third year in medical college, I travelled to see the country with a couple of friends. Our first stop was Calcutta. When I got down at Howrah Railway Station and saw people living on roads in abject poverty, my earlier notion about the supremacy of Andhra civilisation found instant validation. Even in those days Calcutta was chaotic, cluttered with appalling housing, colossal unemployment, shabby roads littered with garbage. We sat down in a rickshaw—a cart pulled by man. Harnessed between the shafts he launches into a perilous trot through the crowded streets. As we passed through Chinatown with its Chinese butchers and shoemakers I vaguely recalled film scenes of mandarins tossing firecrackers at the rickshaw puller's feet to urge him on. But here it would be a waste of time. The congestion of people, carts, lorries, cars, cows and beggars was too dense. Inured as one becomes to poverty and squalor, I was stunned by the chaos and desperation. The plight of the poor is often dignified, almost beautiful, but in Calcutta it was neither. Always it is tragic but the loss of dignity, the debasement of the human spirit, was somehow new and infinitely more horrifying. In Visakhapatnam, it was surreptitiously that an old woman would delve into the rubbish but here whole families were crawling about in piles of refuge seemingly left out for them on purpose. In broad daylight and without shame children fought over a coconut husk or snatched from their mother a rotting banana. Back in Andhra, when the food runs out the people wait. A deputation sets off to the nearest town to seek help. Those remaining would pray. In Calcutta it seemed that such patience and resignation had been forgotten. The city had taught people a different way of life. Survival, like success, is something to be fought for. The enemy is not fate or some evil spirit but your neighbour. Resentment, bitterness and intolerance, attitudes seldom found in rural Andhra, seemed to be the order of the day here. We also visited Santiniketan to see my artist friend Ratnam. The serenity of the place and the cultural richness in the air was amazing at the least. I wondered why Bengal was a land of contrasts. Were people living on roads as animals essential for the existence of a *Bhadralok* oasis?

From Calcutta, we went to Benares. There, I stayed with my friend C.S. Rao. Benares is one of the few places where the Ganges has settled for a regular course. Deserting its predominantly south-easterly flow it swings north and up past the holy city. On the right-hand bank there are the usual sand dunes and flat wasteland but on the left rise the famous bathing ghats and above them a chaotic skyline of tall palaces, temple *sikharas,* even minarets and Buddhist pagodas with the occasional glimpse of a golden spire. The sun rises out of the flat wasteland in the east. First, like the solitary spotlight, it strikes the minaret and golden spire, then the palaces and temples and slowly down the steep *ghats* to the water's edge. This is the moment for spiritual renewal. Almost bare bodies, old and young, fat and thin, plunged into the momentarily sparkling waters. Females, draped in their wet *saries,* remain close to the shore. The air is filled with the hum of prayer and away towards Dufferin Bridge goes a flotilla of jasmine and marigold flowers, the offerings of the faithful.

Up and down in front of the *ghats* glide an assortment of craft, rowing boats and big two-tired motor launches packed with sightseers. Like cruising crocodiles they pause to feint with opened jaws before a plump Bengali lady in trouble with her billowing sari standing motionless with a pot of *ganga jal* raised to the sun. For me it was too much like sacrilege. Our boatman pulled obligingly upstream for a closer look at the less commercialised spectacles.

In Benares the threads of Hinduism and of India, like the tangled skein of the Ganges itself, begin to fall into place. The Brahmin, his sacred thread slung diagonally across the body from shoulder to hip and his *tilak,* a hank of long hair, now wet and hanging from crown to nape, is chanting *Gayatri*, most famous of the Vedic verses. Nearby a *sadhu* with long matted hair, his body smeared with ash and his eyes glazed by narcotics, sits cross-legged and motionless. Across his knees is a trident to distinguish him as a follower of Lord Siva, to whom the city of Benares is dedicated. But sectarianism stops there. In the holy city everyone has a place.

There is a bathing ghat for Muslims, another patronised by Jains, and still more for pilgrims from the South, for Bengalis and for Rajputs. The gilding of the Golden Temple was a courtesy of Maharaja Ranjit Singh, the great emperor of Punjab. The mosque whose minarets pierce the otherwise Hindu skyline is a legacy of the bigoted Aurangzeb. It stands on the site of the temple he destroyed to make way for it. The later ghats are the gifts of great Maratha houses—that of Scindia boasts a wind shelter like those on Eastbound Esplanade. Even if the British never built themselves a ghat there is to the north a far more representative monument, the Dufferin Bridge. Aloof and unconcerned it bears across the sacred river the symbols of the White Man's bounty, the railway and the Grand Trunk Road.

Above the ghats is a maze of narrow streets crowded with cattle and pilgrims. Dodging the piles of holy cow dung a party of Gujarati peasants in heavy clumping shoes and bulky turbans come clattering over the cobbles. They are late for the sunrise. Back home in Saurashtra it rises a good hour later than here. We took rides in a horse-drawn cart whose bumps make you remember your mother's lap and the rhythmic sound of horse taps, her lullabies.

I can still recall, after 50 years the same feeling I faced across a few feet of water, the burning ghats. Two or three funeral pyres were blazing brightly in the morning sun. Another body carried precariously down the steps on a pyre and covered with pink cloth was waiting its turn. Pink means a woman's corpse, said the boatman. Another pyre went up with a dry whoosh of flame, the water lapped at the lower logs and the sun went on shining—an elemental scene. If there is a short cut to Nirvana, I think I had seen that in Benares that morning. Before returning we went to Benares Hindu University. I was thrilled to see the vastness of the university campus. A sense of reverence about the place engulfed my mind.

On another occasion, I detoured South India, mostly Tamil Nadu. Just as the Ganges rises high in the Himalayas so the Kavery, the sacred river of the South, rises in the hills of Coorg. It flows south-east past Mysore City, into the R.K. Narayan country and so lazily into the rich coastal plain near Trichi and Tanjore. Here one is in a land as hallowed as the Gangetic plain. Although it was in the North that the Sanskrit roots of Hinduism spread into the Indian soil, much of its subsequent growth has taken place in the South. The famous saints Sankaracharya, Ramanuja and Madhavacharya to whom can be attributed the prominence of Siva, Vishnu, and Krishna in the modern Hindu pantheon were all South Indian Brahmins. Tamil and other South Indian languages have a richer religious and devotional literature than any other modern Indian tongue.

The vast temple complexes are thronged with people. In the temple at Madurai the offering box was a giant iron safe embedded in the stone floor. Within its precincts is a bazaar where one can buy pots and pans, baskets, bangles and anklets as well as every conceivable devotional aid—statues, rosariers, joss sticks, bells, oil lamps, flowers and fruits. The air was thick with the smell of jasmine and bananas. In the temple pool devout ladies were washing themselves and their saries without the least indecency.

I found people in Tamil Nadu generally rude and arrogant. The finesse of Andhra was totally missing. The *pan* spitting habit prevalent there was particularly disturbing. The North and South India are two different realities but for the common religion that binds them. North Indians carve their deities in marble to boast of their fair complexion, a reminiscence of their Aryan ancestry. South Indians make their deities in granite to reflect their Dravidian roots. Though Hindu religion places the Gita, which talks about omnipresent formless supreme God at its ideological centre—masses flock temples and prostrate before idols and highly ornamented images of the God.

Back at home, on September 15, 1948, Lakshmi gave birth to our first child, a daughter. The delivery took place in the Mission Hospital at Vuyyur, 10 miles from Pedamuttevi. I visited them later and saw in my child divine grace and charm personified. We named her Sabitha.

In college, the course work was over and I started internship at the King George Hospital. I was fast learning to be a doctor, someone who finds a fault, evolves a solution and eventually delivers it. The human body and its problems were drawing me deep into their almost mystical world. One day, we were having an appendix removal procedure. Prof Atma Rama Rao was in command. He made a small insertion in the abdomen and asked me to remove the appendix. Hardly had I put my fingers when Prof Atma Rama Rao commented that with such a big hand I was better suited to be in a motor garage than in the Operation Theatre. The comment was rude and unfounded in the first place. Abdomen was my favourite zone in human anatomy, a total wonderland. The abdominal cavity contains the liver, stomach, intestines, spleen, pancreas, and kidneys. In the lower part of the abdomen, enclosed by the pelvis, are the bladder, rectum, and in women, the uterus and ovaries. With ultrasound imaging not yet arrived, little was known about the precise location of this heavily crowded place in the human body. Without allowing the insult hurled at me by an arrogant teacher to disrupt my mind-body harmony, I performed the procedure with finesse of which I was always very proud.

I completed my internship in 1951. Two opportunities opened up—one in the Army for Short Service Commission as a Medical Officer and the other in the form of an advertisement from the Indian Medical Association (IMA) inviting doctors willing to serve in the USA. I applied for both and went to Delhi with Dr. Papa Rao. We first appeared for the Service Commission. They selected Papa Rao and rejected me. So, I approached IMA without any other option. Playing safe, I offered my services in the areas of Radiology or alternatively, Dermatology, both of which considered as inferior to glamorous disciplines of surgery and general medicine and would thus invite lesser competition. I was selected as a Radiologist.

Dr. S.C. Sen interviewed me at IMA. He was settled in the UK and was married to a Jewish lady. In typical Bengali hyperbola, Dr. Sen presented an irresistible picture of the land of opportunity that the USA was and pointed towards the sky to tell me how far could I go professionally if I worked there.

I returned to Visakhapatnam, wound up there and reached Pedamuttevi. More than 200 people gathered in front of our house. My father and brothers felt proud. Lakshmi was understandably silent and serious. My father-in-law gave me Rs. 4000. I sat in a cart with Lakshmi and my two uncles from her side, Anjaneyulu and Kutumba Rao and reached Nidumolu. From there we took a bus to Vijayawada. There we boarded a train to Madras. Here, Lakshmi and Anjaneyulu saw us off. I went to Bombay with Kutumba Rao who was familiar with the city. By the time steamship *SS Stretheden* sailed off Bombay for Southampton in England, I was fully tired. A poem of William Shakespeare was prominently painted on the wall in the cafeteria in the ship:

'There is a tide in the affairs of men
Which taken at the flood, leads on to fortune:
Omitted, all the voyage of their life
Is bound in shallow and in miseries.

I felt pain, sorrow, and grief over going away from those who were mine but there was hope too. I knew for many years now I would be living on hopes and memories. Man looks forward with smiles but backwards with sighs. What a wise providence of God! The cup of life is sweetest at the brim, the flavour is impaired as we drink deeper, and the dregs are made bitter so that we may not struggle when it is taken away from our lips.

□

3

The vastness of the sea was amazing. The smallness of man and his creations had suddenly become so obvious that I found myself sunk in despair. Hardly a day had passed when I felt myself living in the solitude of a limbo for an eternity. I had uprooted myself from the place I belonged to and not yet arrived anywhere to strike my roots. The self had become so meaningless in the absence of others. I had a habit of distinguishing experience in different ways. I would regard part of all I experience at any time and place as 'me' and the rest as 'not me'. I think of me being inside my body and at the same time the inside of my body being somehow 'inside' my private space. As someone had said, "Bitter would have me taste: my taste was I."

Was I missing anything? No. I had never found myself at ease with my people. I was an alien within the social fantasy system of Pedamuttevi. I always believed, and do so even today, that no one would experience my experience and that everyone relies on communications to understand how or what I am thinking, feeling, imagining, dreaming, and so forth. And this is true the other way also. My feelings about others originate from my interpretation of other's feelings because as no one can experience what I am experiencing. How could I experience someone else's experiences. With no one around, I would stretch on the deck and search my reference co-ordinates in vain alternately in the immensity of sky above and the sea below.

There were many European Buildings in Bandar; many of them built by the Portuguese who arrived in India earlier than the British and the French. When Vasco de Gamma reached Calicut in 1499, he sailed for over two years from Lisbon to India circling the African continent. Then, when European nations subjugated and colonised parts of Asia as a short cut, Suez Canal was excavated during 1859-69 across the great Arabian Desert in Egypt linking the Red Sea with the Mediterranean. While crossing the Suez Canal, my depression finally overcame my body resistance and I fell sick. It took nine days for the ship to reach the port of Gibraltar in Spain, where the Mediterranean opens into the Atlantic Ocean. On disembarking, I virtually ran away from the ship. However, it didn't take me long to realise that it was not my land. I wanted to drink some fresh water but could not get that anywhere around. I was offered wine instead. Fortunately, our Spanish halt was meant only for a day and when the ship sailed for the Southampton port of England I was much stronger and stable, if not physically, at least mentally.

At Southampton, we changed over to a liner named Queen Mary. It was a big ship with multiple floors, spacious and royal in splendour. It sailed faster too. We were told that all it would take a week to cross the Atlantic. A group of Asian doctors boarded the ship at Southampton and the focus shifted to professional discussions pulling me out of my depression. There was plenty of entertainment and good food. In each meal, we were served different dishes from different parts of the world. We had rice with Thai curry, Korean curry, Japanese curry, Indonesian curry, including my own Indian curry. There were lots of fruits, desserts, and of course drinks.

One afternoon, we were lazing on the deck. I ate one apple and was about to throw the core, when an elderly British lady, sitting by my side, anticipated my action and very kindly gave me a paper napkin. There was no offence, no arrogance, only pure grace. I wrapped the core in the napkin and kept it in my pocket for throwing it into the waste bin later. I had always been very tidy and clean. This lesson graduated me to the newer heights of refined manners and etiquette.

The sight of Statue of Liberty was great. Approaching New York through the basin of River Hudson passing through the great monument erected by French engineer Eiffel filled me with a desire to do something that would be as settled and elevated as this statue in the turbulence and impermanance of time.

Symbolically, if not geographically, New York City is at the centre of things—the very definition of a metropolis, or *mother-city.* It is the single place that most encompasses all the shades of the American experience. It is situated where New York Bay and the Hudson, Harlem, and East rivers join. Equidistant from Boston and Washington D.C., New York is the hub of the eastern seaboard.

Five districts locally called as boroughs—Bronx, Brooklyn, Staten Island, Queens and Manhattan—comprise New York City. Each of these boroughs is distinctive, but it is Manhattan with its commanding skyline that stands out in the minds of New Yorkers and non-New Yorkers alike. Only about 20 per cent of New York residents, however, live in Manhattan. I went to Bronx, which is north of Queens and east of Manhattan.

The Bronx Hospital was a Jewish hospital with no great facilities or any learning environment. It didn't take much time for me to understand Dr. Sen's commitment to the Jewish community firmly secured in his wedlock. I was offered a monthly salary of 50 Dollars with free accommodation and food. The whole day would go in examining, studying and diagnosing various ailments with the help of radiological investigations. On the first day we were served ox tongue at the dinner table. It was too much of an ethical shock for me. In spite of the best of efforts to adapt myself to the new environment, I could not relish the regimen. There was an African lady in charge of the mess who would be very kind and considerate to me. She would unfailingly leave one sandwich and a banana in the refrigerator so that I could carry it to the hospital as lunch. On days she would be away from the work, I would be missing my lunch. I didn't know at that time that for the next one year I would be eating boiled rice with sour cream at dinner.

Bronx is a borough of contrasts. South Bronx is a symbol of American poverty with people living in ghettos. Not a day goes without a fire incident. The area's desolation, arson, gangs and drug dealers, among other problems, represent the ugly face of America. With good families having left Bronx for better life in the suburbs, left behind is an increasingly poor population in an area packed with abandoned lots and buildings. In the same borough, however, tree lined Riverdale and Fieldston remain two of New York's most elegant neighbourhoods. About a quarter of the borough's land consists of parks, notably the New York Botanical Garden and the famous Bronx Zoo.

I used to spend all my free time in exploring Manhattan, a complete world within an area of just 4 by 20 kilometre. At every level Manhattan teems with activity. On 10,000 kilometres of city streets, more than 11,000 taxicabs circulate. Above street level some of the world's tallest buildings create self-contained cities in the sky. I was nothing but amazed to see the Empire State Building and the Chrysler Building. Below ground is another city with 200 kilometres of subway routes and separate underground villages of Rockefeller Centre, Grand Central and Pennsylvania stations.

The elevated and serrated skyline is Manhattan's signature—whether viewed from across the bridges in Queens and Brooklyn, the harbour in Staten Island, or the docks of New Jersey. A friend told me that it is durable Manhattan schist, or crystalline rock, whose strength has allowed builders to raise some of the world's tallest structures here. Outcroppings of this rock can be seen poking through the soil in Manhattan's Central Park. The two greatest districts of tall buildings—the densely packed skyscrapers of the financial district in lower Manhattan and the slightly more eclectic towers of Midtown—coincide with the geologic layout of supporting rock.

As goes the local lore, Manhattan was settled from the south, with the Dutch colonists first taking up residence in a fortified encampment near the present-day Battery—so named for its emplacements of cannon. Lower Manhattan is now the financial district. The symbolic as well as geographic centre of this compact district—where streets may be dark all day from the closely spaced tall buildings—is Wall Street, so named because of the fortification built on its present-day course by the Dutch in 1653 to protect against English encroachment.

Walking the Manhattan's roads, laid down as a well-measured

grid, can be a lifetime activity. The logic of right angles—the legacy of mid-19th century city planning is striking. All numbered streets, from 14th past 190th, run approximately east to west, while the broader avenues, from East End to Twelfth, run roughly north to south. Fifth Avenue divides west from east, with all numbered street addresses originating from that point.

Just above 14th Street and west of Fifth Avenue is Chelsea, dotted with large cooperative apartment buildings. To the east of Fifth are the grand old high-rises of Gramercy Park, not far from the city's flower- market district, and the huge apartment complexes of Stuyvesant Town and Peter Cooper Village next to the East River. These buildings were designed to provide middle-income housing for returning World War II servicemen.

Beyond these neighbourhoods, which have remained stable amid surrounding decline, is Midtown. It is Midtown that best exemplifies the urban character of the city. In just one square mile, the size of many suburban shopping malls, Midtown encompasses everything from the old Hell's Kitchen—a once-dangerous slum turned uneasy mixture of office buildings, pornographic shops, and legitimate theatres—to distinctive skyscrapers, elegant boutiques, stately hotels, the monumental New York Public Library, the United Nations, and the city-within-a-city Rockefeller Centre. The centre, created by the oil baron John D. Rockefeller, Jr., is a maze of office buildings, shops, vast underground arcades, the world's largest theatre (Radio City Music Hall, seating 6,000), and in winter an outdoor skating rink. A quarter of a million people pass through the centre each day.

At the northern edge of Midtown's commercial streets begins Central Park, an 800-acre respite that divides Manhattan's Upper West and Upper East sides. While the park appears sylvan and natural, it was in fact wholly designed by the landscape architects Frederick Law Olmsted and Calvert Vaux. Begun in the mid-19th century, the park's deceptively simple layout of glades, lakes, woods and meandering paths took 20 years to complete and required the movement of 10 million cartloads of stone, earth, and topsoil.

North of Central Park the landscape of Manhattan changes

dramatically. On the East Side above 96th Street is East, or Spanish, Harlem. This much blighted area of tenements is predominantly Hispanic (Puerto Rican) and has, through successive immigrant migrations, housed only the poor. To the west is Central Harlem, a once well-to-do neighbourhood that features some of New York's most beautiful brownstones, spacious tree-lined avenues, and such tidy middle-class precincts as Sugar Hill, Strivers Row, with its townhouses designed by Stanford White, and the Gold Coast. Harlem's predominantly black population engages in rich community life that belies its stereotypical image as a crime-ridden slum, though poverty is plainly etched on the neighbourhood's excess of abandoned and decayed buildings.

Farther west are Morning-side Heights and Columbia University. The university's gracious buildings and the huge nearby Episcopal Cathedral of St. John the Divine (only two thirds completed but still the largest Gothic cathedral in the world) are in stark contrast to the surrounding raggedness. Above Harlem and Morning-side Heights, Manhattan Island narrows. Washington Heights and Inwood, making up the northern tip, were once mostly Irish, German and Jewish. By the 1980s, however, this area had become an extension of Harlem, densely populated with blacks, Puerto Ricans, and recent Latino immigrants.

In stark contrast to this horn of plenty is the other New York City, in which 15 per cent of all families live below the poverty level—the highest such percentage in the United States. With poverty have come related problems. Illiteracy (with almost half of the children being school dropouts) and drug abuse (particularly the long-standing menace of heroin and the highly potent "crack" form of cocaine) keep many of the city's poorest residents away from the doors of opportunity. That there exist in the midst of all that wealth and opportunity such barriers as racism, declining industrial employment and the lack of vocational training was a real eye opener. At the very lowest level of poverty, the warm subway gates and building lobbies of New York were filled with homeless persons and families. "As many as 100,000 persons spend each winter night on the streets," I read in a newspaper. How nicely poet OW Holmes had written:

Build thee more stately mansions, O, my soul
As the swift seasons roll!
Leave thy low-vaulted past!
Let each new temple, nobler than the last
Shut thee from heaven with a dome more vast,
'Till thou at length art free,
Leaving thine outgrown shell by life's unresting sea!

Most of my patients were blacks or working class, non-elite struggling Americans. One day, I was about to pack up when I saw a heavy built American patient smiling at me. It was a thin forced smile but nevertheless attracted me. I walked to his bed and asked how he was doing. His name was Matthew. He obviously wanted to engage himself in some conversation with someone to allay some of his inner fears. Whatever it was, he didn't get much chance to mull that over. As I sat down at his bedside, he suddenly threw his head back and bellowed out a wordless roar that seemed to rise up out of his throat from somewhere deep within his stricken heart. He hit his balled fists with startling force up against the front of his chest in a single synchronous thump, just as his face and neck, in the flash of an instant, turned swollen and purple. His eyes seemed to have pushed themselves forward in one bulging thrust, as though they were trying to leap out of his head. He took one immensely long, gurgling breath, and died. A man who was just smiling at me turned into a corpse. Suddenly as if stupefying in its horror, the dead Matthew, whose soul was by that time totally departed, threw back his head once more. Staring upward at the ceiling with the glassy, unseeing gaze of open dead eyes, he roared out to the distant heavens a dreadfully rasping whoop that sounded like the hounds of hell were barking. I looked into its glazed eyes and saw Matthew's pupils fixed in the position of wide black dilatation that signifies brain death, and obviously would never respond to light again. I knew I was seeing the Matthew version of the death rattle, a sound made by spasm in the muscles of the voice box, caused by the increased acidity in the blood of a newly dead man. It was his way, it seemed, of asking doctors to desist from doing anything with him anymore.

Medical science has conferred on humanity the benefit of

separating those pathological processes that are reversible from those that are not, constantly adding to the means by which the balance shifts in favour of sustained life. But modern medicine has also contributed to the misguided fancy by which each of us denies the advent of our own individual mortality. Contrary to the claims of many doctors, medicine will always remain an art.

One of the most severe demands that the artistry of medicine makes on the physician is that he or she becomes familiar with the poorly delineated boundary zones between categories of treatment whose chances of success may be classified as certain, probable, possible or unreasonable. Those unlit spaces between the probable and everything beyond it are where the thoughtful physician must often grope, with only the wisdom accumulated over a life time to guide him.

When Matthew's life came to its abrupt end, the outcome of his heart was inescapable. Although a great deal had already been understood about heart disease in the early 1950s, the available therapies for it were few and too often inadequate. Matthew died because his heart died. His heart died because it was not getting enough oxygen. It was not getting enough oxygen because it was not getting enough haemoglobin, the blood-borne protein whose function is to carry the oxygen. It was not getting enough haemoglobin because it was not getting enough blood. It was not getting enough blood because the heart's nourishing vessels, the coronary arteries, were hardened and narrowed by a process called arteriosclerosis (literally, hardening of arteries in Greek). The arteriosclerosis had occurred because of a combination of Matthew's sybaritic diet, his cigarette smoking, his lack of exercise, an element of high blood pressure and a certain degree of inherited predisposition. The nurse in charge later told me that in the afternoon Matthew's pampered daughter had called him. The call would have made the same spasm-inducing effect on his severely narrowed coronary arteries as it did on his angrily clenched fists. That bit of acute tightening was probably just enough to rupture or crack one of the deposits of arteriosclerosis, yellowish plaques of cholesterol, lipids and cellular debris, in the inner layers of the walls of large and medium sized coronary arteries. Once this occurred, the disrupted plaque served as a focus on which fresh blood clots formed, making the obstruction complete and choking off the already-compromised flow. This final stoppage caused the so-called Ischemia, or blood-lack, thereby acutely starving a large-enough piece of Matthew's heart muscles, or myocardium, to disrupt its normal rhythm into the chaotic squirming of ventricular fibrillation.

It is quite possible that Matthew's heart muscle was not actually killed by its acute blood lack. Holding back of blood, called Ischemia by doctors *(Ischein* is *to hold back* and *haema* is *blood* in Greek) alone may cause ventricular fibrillation, especially in a heart already injured by a previous attack. Adrenaline-like compounds produced by the body at the time of stress could also have caused fibrillation. Whatever the cause, the electrical communication system upon which Matthew's heart depended for its regularity and co-ordination broke down, and so did Matthew's life.

More and more Matthews are found these days. They are betrayed by their eating, smoking and their inattention to such simple housekeeping chores as exercise and the maintenance of normal blood pressure. Sometimes pedigree alone gives them away, in the form of family history or diabetes. It may also be because of a driving impetuosity and aggressiveness that today's cardiologists call the *Type A* personality. In a way, the person whose heart muscle will be anguished by angina (from the Latin word *angor quinsy* which means strangling) is very like the overly ambitious schoolchild who throws a hand aggressively into the air when the teacher looks for volunteers—"Choose me, choose me. I can do it better than anyone else." He is easy to identify, and death will easily single him out. There is little randomness in the choices made by the cardiac ischemia. You can easily identify people running towards a cardiac death by their speedometers.

There is a very interesting paradox in modern medicine. The holistic thought process I attempted to demonstrate through the story of the Matthew's heart above would not have become possible without dispassionate observation. The introduction of three instruments in the nineteenth century did much to redirect the path of medical progress away from clinical artistry and toward the goal of scientific objectivity. In 1819, the stethoscope was introduced and the very first distancing took place, both literal and symbolic, between doctor and patient. In 1830, a newly identified law of optics permitted the correction of an aberration in lenses, thereby making the microscope a useful tool for the first time since its invention in the late seventeenth century. This gave doctors an opportunity to study the minutest and more disembodied bits of their patients. In 1895, Wilhelm Konrad Roentgen discovered X-rays, and the need for the presence of even minute samples of patients lessened, replacing them with a shadowed image imprinted on a photographic emulsion.

Fed up with mere existence at Bronx Hospital and unable to learn much beyond daily chores of reading X-ray films I got enrolled for Masters at the New York University. Though I had opted for Radiology while coming here for reasons nothing to do with any professional interest or love for the subject, by now I started liking the shadows of human interiors. The black and white world of internal reality of human body was both mysterious and esoteric. It was like an arranged marriage with a stranger, who eventually becomes your made-for-each-other life partner. The Rs. 4000 given by my father-in-law were intact with me. It made $ 1000 required for paying the admission fee. For additional recurring expenses, I worked in the Bronx Hospital at nights as a radiology technician for 50 Dollars a month. More as a gesture than recognition of my work in the previous year, the hospital authorities allowed me to retain my room and eat in the hospital cafeteria.

Studying for the Masters and working in the hospital for survival was stressful but rewarding for the real practical education that I was getting in that process. Within months of this dual existence I understood Louis Pasteur's famous saying, "Where observation is concerned chance favours the prepared mind." After spending late evenings with patients I used to be brilliant in the class during the day.

The atmosphere at the University was very stimulating. The teachers were clear about what they were teaching and there was professionalism in the way students and teachers interacted with each other. During the course, I dissected the entire human body and stood first in the examination. A look at the entire human body cut open is never normal even to the hardest professionals in medicine. Bones, tissues, organs, veins, nerves, lymph nodes, all appear so different and yet so similar. From what material do all these things arise?

Students of medicine are still made to recite from memory the Latin phrase uttered by German medical researcher Rudolf Virchow in 1855—omnis cellula e cellula—"every cell originates from a previously existing cell." The creation and continuity of life depend on the cellular reproduction of life already present. The key to the continuity is the equal division into two offspring cells from one parent. In this way, nature ceaselessly duplicates the smallest of its units that are endowed with the potentiality of independent existence.

There are many local environmental conditions that must be met to ensure continued cellular existence and optimal performance of tissues and organs. The stability of the surroundings must be maintained for a body to be healthy and free of disease. French word *milieu inte'rieur* (internal surroundings) so nicely defines interstitial body fluid under which each cell must be bathed at every instant of its life. This fluid provides a medium for the elementary exchange of nutrients and waste materials in and out of the cells. All fundamental processes necessary for the maintenance and life of the tissue elements depend on the stability and balance of this environment.

The approximately 60 trillion cells of the human body, each measuring 50 to 80 microns, one millionth of a meter in size, make up about two-thirds of its weight. The structure of any cell is characterised by three predominant features. There is an enveloping membrane that, like a casing or skin, demarcates the cell from everything around it. Then, there is the nucleus, containing the genetic material—deoxyribonucleic acid or DNA and, assorted material filling the cell body collectively called cytoplasm.

The membrane is a thin, all encompassing barrier having the capability of selecting exactly what it will and will not allow entering or leaving the cell. The membrane is never smooth and no two cells are ever identical. The cells have a wide variety of shapes and geometric forms, depending on their function in the body. In fact, Nature has used the stratagem of providing all manner of in-folds and out-pouches. Cells of certain tissues whose main function is absorption, such as those of intestines and gall bladder, have even finger-like outgrowths. Irrespective of its contours, a cell membrane is always composed of a flexible double layer of an oleginous kind of fatty material, or lipid, whose consistency can be compared to that of a light grade of machine oil.

Protein molecules float in nanometer, one billionth of a meter thick membrane, in such a way that most of the times if their one end is in, the other is out. When the concentration of pressure of particles on one side of the membrane is higher than on the other, the two sides tend to become equalised by such passive means as diffusion or osmosis. But when the needs of the cell demand that the substances enter or leave against the pressure or concentration gradient, an active form of transport requiring energy takes place through the embedded protein channels. This uses up to 40 per cent of a cell's energy supply. Bacteria are engulfed into the cell, in a process called endocytosis by biologists. In the opposite process of exocytosis, blisterlike byproducts of cell-metabolism are expelled through membranes. In fact, membranes of each individual cell are crucial participants in the series of tactics by which entire organisms—you and I—adapt to the constant flux of conditions around them and within them.

The cell is in fact the sphere of influence of its nucleus. It is enclosed within a double membrane, perforated at intervals by numerous pores that allow various substances to enter and leave. The nucleus contains a large number of loosely coiled threadlike fibres of a material called chromatin which, during the process of reproduction, coil more tightly and are then called chromosomes, forty-six in number for humans. Each chromosome is a single DNA molecule plus a considerable amount of protein material that acts as scaffolding. Were it to be unfolded, stretched out, and pinned end to end, all the DNA in a human cell's forty-six chromosomes would measure six feet in length.

It is a good point where I think I should introduce the concept of genes. Genes are biological elements that contain information that can be transmitted from one generation to the next. Each gene, of which each of us have some 30,000, is therefore a unit of heredity. It is made up of a bit of DNA. Each gene is a localised region on the length of the DNA molecule. In fact, only a small fraction of a cell's DNA is composed of genes, probably less than 10 per cent. And so, on the face of it, a gene is neither more nor less than a chemical structure lying somewhere along the DNA molecule. If you are disappointed at the smallness of your great heritage, it is understandable. But this is an area that holds the key to the way medical science will take its course in the twentyfirst century. And in your lifetime itself gene-therapy will replace many costly treatments and create some truly impossible ones. We will come back to it later in the book.

Notwithstanding a boring professional career, people at Bronx Hospital were very kind and good. Dr. Bernstein, the Chief of the Hospital, used to have a special liking for me. He used to lock himself with me in his office to discuss radiographs. In a silent recognition of my talent, the University van would bring wet film and a view box to my room in the odd hours for interpretation and second opinion. Whenever I met him outside the hospital, he would invite me to his house for dinner but almost as a second thought postpone it on some pretext like his wife was fixing new curtains or changing the sofa. I could finally have a dinner at his house in the seventh month since the first invitation.

In one student feat, one smart salesman sold me a pipe, highlighting the bargain of getting an item worth five Dollars for only a Dollar. I smoked the pipe with curiosity and a sense of some false pride that generally goes with exhaling smoke. I found the experience terrible and didn't smoke ever again.

After completing post-graduation I wound up at Bronx Hospital and shifted to Bellevue Medical Centre where I got a fellowship from Picker Foundation for doing research in Radiology. My passion for Radiology was deepening. One day a gentleman came searching for me in the hospital. He introduced himself as Dr. Chamberlain from Philadelphia and interviewed me for a position I applied for. Unlike in India, where a job seeking person is treated like a beggar and the persons on the interview board give vent to their lifetime frustrations through questions hurled at the applicant, I had a pleasant experience here. Dr. Chamberlain was very objective in his queries and was more interested in knowing all that I could do than in what I was doing. I could feel his warmth of appreciation for my knowledge. I was offered a yearly remuneration of 10,000 Dollars. It came like a pleasant morning breeze after a long, humid summer night. I later appeared for National Boards in Radiology and was successful. Then I applied for fellowship in Radiology to Sinai Hospital in Baltimore.

Southwest of New York, Baltimore, the largest city in the State of Maryland and hardly 40 miles away from the United States capital Washington D.C., was highly industrialised. At Sinai Hospital, I was asked to work under Dr. Juliann 0. Salik, a sort of administrator there. There was another Jewish Radiologist with me. He was paid 20,000 Dollars for the same, if not less, work that I was doing. There was unsaid racial discrimination in the system and white skin arrogance among senior doctors. Dr. Salik would dare not say anything to my Jewisn counterpart who used to regally march out exactly at 5 O'clock but would sadistically engage me in the name of discussing films till at least 8 PM. I was amazed at the striking contrast between Dr. Chamberlain and Dr. Salik. Even in a radiograph, between the black of a void and white of a bone, there is a vast gray world of tissues and organs. Between Dr. Chamberlain and Dr. Salik, I thought, the entire American people were represented. If there was anything common between what Dr. Chamberlain offered me at Bellevue and what Dr. Salik actually gave me here, it was an opportunity to learn.

Baltimore was burned to the ground in 1904 except for the domed 1867 City Hall at North Holiday Street. Though the city was quickly rebuilt, the downtown area never recovered its character. I still carry memories of National Aquarium at East Pratt Street, amply stocked with colourful tropical fish, glassy-eyed sharks, dainty seahorses and the like. The City was crazy with baseball and we found Babe Ruth Museum at Emory Street packed with photographs and baseball memorabilia tracing the life and career of this legendary ballplayer enthralling. I saw a couple of baseball games in Oriole Park at Camden Yards, one of baseball's prettiest stadiums in the world thanks to its old-style arches, fancy ironwork and overall classic look. Images of waterfront shopping and dining at Inner Harbour in downtown Baltimore are also alive.

I started socialising by now. This made me meet compatriot Dr. Acharyulu who would boast about his great religious lineage—altruistic and purer than the purest—but miss no opportunity of having a free non-vegetarian feast. In one gathering we were served plain food comprising rice, potatoes and boiled spinach. Acharyulu commented loudly that even cows in his village would not eat the stuff.

And there's a lust in man no charm can tame
Of loudly publishing our neighbour's shame;
On eagles' wings immortal scandals fly,
While virtuous actions are but born and die.

It is generally true that all that is required to make men unmindful of what they owe to God for any blessing is that they should receive that blessing often and regularly. Human affairs are not so happily arranged that the best things please man most. Modesty seldom resides in a breast that is not enriched with nobler virtues. Different shades of foolishness sprang up at his arrogant utterance. There are many definitions of arrogance including the one that says it is imitation of the powerful by the weak.

Having settled down professionally and financially I could now invite Lakshmi. She arrived in the middle of winter in 1953 and had all the problems that anyone else would have had in adjusting to an alien world. While clinging to the forms of the past in India, Indians in the United States, like any other minority anywhere else, experiment. Yet I found that most of them refused to jettison the conventional idea of marriage or the familiar family forms. They continue searching for happiness within the orthodox format.

We used to discuss young Indian families living around. The orthodox Indian format presupposes that two young people will be *arranged* to meet one another and marry. It presupposes that the two will fulfil certain psychological needs of each other, and their personalities will develop over the years, more or less in tandem, so that they continue to fulfil each other's needs. It further presupposes that this process will last 'until death do us part'. These expectations, built deeply into our culture back home, are no longer respectable in contemporary American society. People find it increasingly difficult to marry for anything but love. Love has changed from a peripheral concern of the family into its primary justification. Indeed, the pursuit of love through family life has become, for many, the very purpose of life itself.

Love, in American Society, is defined in terms of this notion of shared growth. It is seen as a beautiful mesh of complementary needs, flowing into and out of one another, fulfilling the loved ones, and producing feelings of warmth, tenderness and devotion. Unhappy husbands often complain that 'they have left their wives behind' in terms of social, educational or intellectual growth. The quality of the relationship between husband and wife is considered dependent upon the 'degree of matching in their phases of distinct but comparable development'. As the life expectancy rose from, say fifty to seventy years, thereby lengthening the term during which this acrobatic feat of matched development is supposed to be maintained, the odds against success become absolutely astronomical. I read to Lakshmi a report from Nelson Foote, a sociologist and specialist on the family, 'To expect a marriage to last indefinitely under modern conditions is to expect a lot. To ask love to last indefinitely is to expect even more." Transience and novelty faced by young Indian couples in the United States were both in league against happiness in their families. Lakshmi used to be a golden ear to many dissatisfied Indian ladies. She would advise them to be like nurses in a battlefield hospital where bruised and battered soldiers return. She would also tell them to anchor their spouses against the storm of change and challenges in this foreign land. Lakshmi adapted herself to American life very fast. She joined interior decoration and music classes and learned several new things and skills like an energetic young student.

Our second child, Janatha, was born in December 1954. To earn some extra money to buy some more comforts for the family I used to work in a blood bank in the evenings at 5 Dollars an hour and on weekends at 25 Dollars a shift. My job was to check the pulse and blood pressure of the donor and prick the needle. We bought a Chevrolet Impala car and started going on long drives. Together with a Taiwanese lady doctor, named Tawan, and an American friend Dr. Freed, we visited 42 restaurants of different nations in the city of New York City in the summer of 1955.

Lakshmi and I made good friends with Elsa, a beautiful colleague of mine and her physicist husband Joe Warmund. They were German Jews with a very painful and tortured past. On Christmas in 1955 we decorated our house as any other Christian would do and hosted dinner for them. To make them happy, I played an LP record of Symphony III presented to us earlier by them. Having listened for a minute, Joe hugged me saying that the record was playing at the wrong speed.

There was a warm feeling about India and Indians in America during those days. Indian Prime Minister Jawaharlal Nehru was a popular personality and his friendship with President Eisenhower used to get good coverage in the media. Many of my patients and American friends used to call me Nehru. American people were in general very kind and helpful but so long as money was not involved. The kindness would give way to coldness, the moment any monetary commitment surfaces. In fact the outward finesse and energy of Americans did not fascinate me. When Dr. Bernstein took me out for coffee and paid only for his drink that cost hardly 10 cents I was literally shocked. Overall, I found Americans are as good or as bad as my own people but for the fact that they give a lot of importance to the present moment. Someone told me, "The past is gone and the future is yet to come. What God gives you is today, that is why it is called *present.*" Between 6 PM and 8 PM, majority of American people, after finishing their occupational work and having an early dinner, would go for some learning activity ranging from dance classes to cookery. It was more because of the American way of life than anything special on my part that I took classes in public speaking and music appreciation, with all my professional and family commitments.

As I got more and more drowned in my work and my other activities aimed at acquiring more skills and adding on to my calibre, Lakshmi started getting isolated and restless. She would miss her parents and long for the familiarity of Pedamuttevi. As poet Byron put it so precisely, there are times in life when you lose interest in your surroundings however lively and good they are:

Society is now one polished horde,
Formed of two mighty tribes,
The Bores and the Bored.

When one door of happiness closes, another opens. But somehow we keep looking at the closed door and not even look at the one which has been opened. Though almost obsessive about excellence and a meaningful life. I had never become insensitive, to the emotions and aspirations of others around me. I can't be brave if only wonderful things happen to me. I can't grow better if everything around me continues to be good and satisfactory. So I take life as it comes to me without any grudge, remorse or dodging. I see some positive aspect in whatever life presents and I always try to take it forward into the future with me. Somewhere both of us together decided to go back to India without much ado and deliberation. The timing had to be made.

Rajkumari Amrit Kaur, a well-known socialite from Delhi and Health Minister of India, visited New York in 1956 with one Dr. Sundaram. They were on the look out for faculty for the All India Institute of Medical Sciences (AIIMS), started by the Government of India to nurture advanced scientific healthcare in the country. They conducted interviews for selection to fill positions. Rajkumari treated me very kindly. There was warmth radiating out of her that could be felt as pride, arrogance or adulation, depending upon its recipient. She gave me a big pep talk about my duty to serve my people by returning to India. How can a *good* person like me ignore her crusade for her people? She wondered. She promised me a good position in the Institute. This had precipitated our return to India in June 1956.

Lakshmi was in her sixth month of pregnancy. Not knowing when or whether we would be coming out to this part of the world again, we decided to stop *en route* at Naples in Italy and have some leisure. I booked my Chevrolet Impala on a cargo ship. It would signify the American grandeur amidst which we had lived all these years for my people back home.

The appreciation of beauty is always heightened by a little danger. When we reached Amalfi coast in Naples, it was the first thought that struck me. This dramatic limestone ridge jutting out from an impossibly blue Mediterranean certainly merits that kind of sharpened awareness. The coast unfolds as a seemingly endless progression of seaside towns surrounded by lemon and olive groves. Irregular grey cliffs plunge from startling heights directly into the sea below, punctuated by renegade clumps of wild flowers and an occasional medieval tower in ruins. According to the ancient Greeks, these cliffs were frequented by the sirens, those alluring demi-women that tempted sailors to blissful oblivion on the perilous rocks below.

We wandered through the steep, narrow streets of the pedestrian zone, watching impeccably dressed couples browse the small boutiques in the failing light. Many shops were draped with racks of the gauzy, hand-dyed clothing the town is famous for; others displayed funky ceramics, fine leather bags and expensive show pieces. And flowers were everywhere—in vases at the door of a little trattoria, clinging to the crumbling wall of an old church, in the arms of a passing girl. Their mingling scents seemed to hover in the still air. Waves of surprising size were pounding the stony shore, forcing the fishermen to pull their pastel-coloured boats to higher ground. Pleasant open-air restaurants surrounded this beach. Their terraces were only about half full at this early hour, but the atmosphere was festive, inviting; their lights reflected far out on the surface of the water. And behind the restaurants, rising almost vertically above their soft incandescent glow, the houses and gardens of *Positano* climbed the face of the darkening cliffside toward a star-less indigo sky. I stopped by and took in as much of this scene as my senses could gather. The pleasures offered by this coast were rather more subtle—the never ending seafood lunch overlooking the cove, the afternoon stroll though the modest but impeccable garden, the discovery of a tiny shrine in the cliff-side where wild flowers and talisman stones surround a picture of Virgin Mary.

There was a game of *kayak* polo being played in the little harbour of Amalfi when we arrived. Two teams of bright-jerseyed men paddled furiously back and forth after a soccer ball, whapping it toward the goals with their oars. The coach of one of the teams shouted from the sidelines, performing an elaborate dance of anger, joy, anxiety and frustration. Dozens of rapt spectators on the quay were watching the coach, not the game. They burst into raucous laughter every time his emotions changed in response to the action on the water below.

As one of the local guidebooks put it: "So intense and unrepeatable is the impression made on the visitor, so emotionally involved does he become, that he abandons himself to the prompting of his own imagination and loses all contact with reality." Well, the Italians have never been known for their gift of understatement, but the vivid green of the grotto was pretty impressive. My favourite part was the cave formations, all of which seemed to resemble—in the eyes of our oarsmen, at least—great figures from Italian history. It was a real good time there. We returned to India flying Air India, which had come into being by then.

□

PART II

Creation

Weariness grips your limbs and within the locked horizons
Dumbly ring the bells of hugely gathering fears.
Still, O bird, O sightless bird,
Not yet, not yet the time to furl your wings.

Rabindranath Tagore

4

We reached Pedamuttevi without any future plans. On August 28, 1956, Lakshmi gave birth to our third daughter at Mission Hospital, Vijayawada. We named her Amita. Leaving Lakshmi and daughters in the care of her parents, I went to Delhi to meet Rajkumari Amrit Kaur and take up her *good* offer at the All India Institute of Medical Sciences. It was a real heartbreaking experience to find Rajkumari out of power. With her fade-out, the Institute authorities found me hardly of any interest and in fact informed me with stupid arrogance that they didn't even recognise American medical degrees. More than that, my dreams of settling into a rewarding career in my country were dashed. It was a rude shock to my professional pride. Almost instantly I turned frustrated and indescribably wearied.

"When it is dark enough, men see the stars." The wise words of Ralph Waldo Emerson pulled me through the all-uphill road I was trudging. I decided to take everything positively and landed in Hyderabad to explore any other possibilities of surviving with dignity. The most vital test of a man's character lies not in how he behaves after success, but how he survives defeat. We stayed in Hotel Royal in Nampally. I was very impressed by the roads, gardens and orderly life in Hyderabad and almost fell in love with the city. The air was filled with a lazy serenity that was more contagious than soothing. My old friend Dr. Papa Rao invited me to join his Nursing Home at Cherukaupally, ten miles from Tenali. But by then I had already made up mind to make Hyderabad my home. Man must be arched and buttressed from within. Who else can stop him from biting the dust?

On October 30, 1956, after a month-long fruitless search for a proper place to start, I met Mehdi Nawaz Jung, a local chieftain. One—Dr. Syed Ali, who was present, offered his unsolicited opinion that in America postgraduate medical degrees are served in cocktail parties to the favoured ones or for a price. Impressed by my candour but unable to look beyond the horizon presented by Dr. Syed Ali, Mehdi Nawaz Jung made me an Honorary Radiologist at the Osmania Hospital on a princely honorarium of one Rupee a month. I truly thanked him and decided to join with honest humility. The world has a way of giving what is expected of it. If you are frightened and anticipate failure, you will get it no matter how hard you try to succeed. Lack of faith in yourself and, in what life will do for you cuts you off from the good things of the world. Expect victory and you make victory. Nowhere is this truer than in professional life, where bravery and faith bring both material and spiritual rewards.

On November 1, 1956 in accordance with the recommendations of the States Reorganisation Commission, the Andhra State was enlarged by the addition of nine districts formerly in the Nizam's Dominion. The new State consisted of three distinct regions: coastal region, comprising nine districts, generally called Andhra, the interior region, consisting of four districts collectively known as Rayalaseema and Telengana region, consisting of the capital Hyderabad and these nine districts. N. Sanjeeva Reddy took over as the Chief Minister of Andhra Pradesh. The bureaucracy as well as its ways, however, remained by and large the same.

Though I held only an honorary position in the Osmania General Hospital, I would reach there at 8 AM and remain there for almost ten hours with an hour's break for lunch with Lakshmi at home. Irrespective of my self-motivated efforts and drive, the honorary job hardly demanded much of my professional skill. Sustaining this routine for almost six months, I decided to do something more meaningful by starting my own Radiology clinic. With Dr. Papa Rao, I scouted King's Way, now Rashtrapati Road, in Secunderabad, a distinctly different city from Hyderabad in those days, and hired a premises on a monthly rent of Rs. 300. I sold a part of my share of ancestral land in Pedamuttevi for Rs. 50,000 and bought an X-ray machine from Siemens against outright cash payment. Now, after lunch at home, I would come to the clinic rather than extending my unsolicited self-indulgence in the Osmania Hospital. Finding my Cheverolet Impala out of place in the realm of my present life I sold it off to Akkeneni Nageswara Rao, a well-known cinema hero. I had the pleasure of seeing the car later in many films with some beautiful heroines warming its seats and rubbing their silk with its tapestry.

It was a fateful day in March 1957. I was not well and taking Dibistine tablets. Leaving the bottle under my pillow, I went into the toilet. Janatha, then two years old, came looking for me and finding me inside the toilet started playing on the bed. She discovered the bottle and her curiosity made her open the lid and consume all the tablets inside. When I came out of the toilet I saw a frightening look on her face and discovered to my horror the empty bottle. We rushed her to the Santi Nursing Home in Maredpally for a stomach wash, called gastric lavage, in medical terms.

She was gazing at me and beyond me. Her vague glance was very expressive of emotions penetrating my most inner-self. Her head had fallen back. She was breathing very slowly. The antihistamine drug was slowing down her central nervous system that governs the activities of involuntary muscles, blood vessels, and glands. The toxicity of the ammonium compound now in her blood impaired her brain's function to return appropriate instructions to her circulatory organs.

The autonomic nervous system governs the activities of involuntary muscles, blood vessels and glands. The word autonomic derives from the fact that the system seemingly acts autonomously of conscious will. It consists of nerve cells and fibres of two differently functioning types, comprising what are called the sympathetic and parasympathetic systems. The two parts balance each other's effects in the interest of maintaining the body's homeostatis. The parasympathetic system keeps things slow and steady. In general, it takes care of the regular housekeeping functions of humdrum life, like normal intestinal movements and the dependable beat of the heart. In general, centres in the medulla govern these activities. The sympathetic system, on the other hand, is the one designed to leap into action when certain urgent demands appear, as in excitement. It tends to inhibit the general upkeep function of the parasympathetic system while it takes over to respond to sudden dangerous or exhilarating stimuli. Centres in the hypothalamus govern it.

Almost paralyzed, I was seeing my child sinking into a deep sleep. Sitting as helpless as Lakshmi, I was recalling what was written in my Medicine books as the most open secret of human life: "Man is an obligate aerobe." The dependence on air of all mankind, and indeed all known terrestrial animals, was recognised by primitive tribesmen long before any of them distinguished themselves from their fellows by being called healers. Whatever be the technological sophistication of ultramodern molecular research and the increasingly abstruse terminology of its current literature, the circle of knowledge always returns to its starting point: In order to live, man must have air. We have no choice—without oxygen, our cells die and we die with them. With the lungs not being asked to fill in oxygen and blood vessels not pushing the blood through circulation, Janatha's desperate heart started beating faster to pump more and more blood to her beleaguered cells. After fighting a losing battle against non-responding feed-back circulation, her heart gave up its effort of providing her brain cells their survival ration of oxygen. She had gone from obtundation to minimal responsiveness as her organs failed. We had gone from worry, to despair, and finally to helplessness in the face of destiny. Janatha left us. Some souls visit this world on a real brief sojourn. They are good souls with not much to suffer. However, their departure often leaves those around them with a life long pain.

Oh threats of Hell and Hopes of Paradise!
One thing at least is certain—This life flies;
One thing is certain, and the rest is Lies;
The flower that once has blossom forever dies.

Those were very hard days. For almost a year, I hardly had any practice. The Siemens salesman who sold me the X-ray machine would drop in to see if I am able to use his machine and finding nothing different from his last visit spend a few hours giving company to the idling Radiologist from the United States. I later bought a chessboard to fill my hours in the clinic. Most of the practising doctors had their clinics in Hyderabad and their patients were not willing to spend Rs. 5 on travel to get their X-ray done in my clinic. Many months I ended up paying rent and electricity charges out of my earlier savings. My father-in-law would visit me almost every fortnight on the slightest pretext and bring provisions from village as a silent help to the struggling family. Knowing it well, many relatives would ask my father-in-law about the money I was making out of my *roaring* practice. Insult is deadly when inflicted upon injury. Poet Samuel Johnson expressed it so beautifully:

Of all the grieves that harass the distressed,
Sure the bitterest is a scornful jest;
Fate never wounds more deep the generous heart,
Than when a blockhead's insult points the dart.

At some stage in our evolution, human beings developed a psychological defence system against emotional pain. This allows us to push memories which trigger difficult feelings from the forefront of our conscious mind into the recesses of the subconscious. It is often an essential short-term survival mechanism. It enables us to postpone the healing of our hurt so that we can get on coping with the practical consequences of the hurt, or just carry on surviving in spite of it. I was continuing to earn a living after all these setbacks and disappointments, heckling and criticism. In the only way I knew how to deal with people, I was on a repression spree.

Repression, in its medical sense, is a brilliant emotional management tool, as long as the hurt is given healing attention in the not-too-distant future. The problem arises when it is used as an alternative to healing. Even more problems arise when it becomes a habitual way of dealing with emotional hurt.

Many patients arrive at hospitals for treatment of some disease as emotional pressure cookers with their steam vent choked and about to burst. It is important to remember that the longer our feelings have been repressed, the more difficulty we are likely to have in the healing process. I found it very true in cases where the hurt carried by patients had been very severe. Many of them had locked away the abuse they suffered in early childhood, accidental deaths of parents or siblings, matrimonial incompatibilities in the vaults of their minds so securely that they became notoriously hard to recall. I am amazed to see an almost suicidal trait among Indian adults of denying themselves comfort. Based on my observation of restless and stubborn patients I could identify certain root causes of their resistance to comfort and sadistic enjoyment of their sickness. A majority of them were hurt as a child, having been let down by someone who was supposed to be the comforter like an inadequate or abusive parent. Some had disloyal spouses, friends and hypocritical teachers. Almost all had low self-esteem. They habitually neglected friendships. They lamented their misjudging of friends, having the wrong kind of friends, absence of an appropriate friend and lack of assertiveness.

In an interesting development, the son of Lakshmanaswamy Mudaliar, the doyen of medical education in Madras, returned to India with a post-graduate board diploma in Urology from the United States. Of what relevance are the laws if they cross the dynasty of the king and hinder the march of their offspring? In a jiffy, the Government recognised American Post-graduate degrees. When the Sun shines all get basked. There was nothing left in between an academic position and me in India. I finally entered the faculty in the Osmania Medical College after standing out for no fault of mine for two years. Wise words from Rudyard Kipling:

If you can trust yourself when all men doubt you,
But make allowance for their doubting too;
If you can wait and not be tired by waiting,
And yet don't look too good, nor talk too wise;
Your is the Earth and everything that's in it,
And- which is more-you'll be a Man!

The non-viability of the King's Way clinic was getting more and more confirmed with the passage of time. I sold another chunk of my land in Pedamuttevi and bought a house in Abids area of Hyderabad. I also bought a portable X-ray machine and opened a second clinic in a portion of my new house. Sharing my time between hospital and my two clinics, however, didn't work out well leading to the winding up of the King's Way clinic. By now, worried about the ways of their son-in-law, Lakshmi's parents decided to sell off all their land in the village and migrate to Hyderabad. They purchased land at Toli Chowki, on the western outskirts of the city, and developed a grape garden there.

My father-in-law, a hard worker indeed, would perennially curse the dry land of Hyderabad and the lethargy among local labourers. We certainly felt more secure and comfortable with them around. On November 6, 1959, Lakshmi gave birth to our fourth child, a son. We named him Sushrut.

The Osmania General Hospital was one of the premier medical institutions in the country. Equipped with the best of machines and manned by the best of talent available, it was the place where the rich and powerful would come for their treatment. I was invited by His Highness the seventh Nizam of Hyderabad Mir Osman Ali to carry out his health check.

The Qutb Shahis of Golconda laid the foundations of the modern city of Hyderabad. In 1687, the son of the Mughal emperor Aurangzeb routed the Qutb Shahis and seized Golconda. He appointed Asaf Jah the governor of Deccan. As the Mughal Empire tottered under Aurangzeb's successors, the Asaf Jahis declared themselves independent rulers under the title of Nizam. Five years after Aurangzeb died in 1707, the Viceroy of Hyderabad declared independence and established the Asaf Jahi dynasty of the Nizams. In return for allying with the British against Tipu Sultan of Mysore, the Nizam was allowed to retain a certain degree of autonomy even after the British had come to dominate all India. The Nizams became involved in the Anglo-French wars in the Deccan and had finally to enter into a subsidiary alliance with the British in 1800.

Many ex-rulers could also never quite cope with the realities of a different, democratic India. The fabulous Nizam of Hyderabad sank into miserable isolation. He had a diminutive personality with a feeble voice. He wore cotton pyjamas and *lalchi.* I found him very polite, humble and friendly. There was a grace in his simplicity. Notwithstanding his frail structure, his major faculties were very sound. It will not be out of place to mention here that after his death, his grandson and successor Mukaram Jah, the eighth

Nizam, hounded by tax officials, greedy relatives and deceitful acolytes fled to manage a sheep farm in western Australia. After that venture ended in disaster with his second wife, an Australian, he tried to find his roots again in Hyderabad, changed wives two more times, and now lives mostly in Europe.

Another prominent personality I met during those days was P.V. Narsimha Rao, the learned education minister in the Andhra Pradesh Government. He used to bring his wife who was suffering from a cardiac ailment. I would have taken more than 50 ECGs of the lady. The sagacious figure of Narsimha Rao accompanying his wife with a detached affection was a role model for any middle aged Indian married couple.

There were more than 800 beds, neatly kept and cared. The treatment offered by the Osmania General Hospital was free. Though the Government made provision for charging affluent patients, most of them preferred paying doctors in their home clinics and get free treatment in the hospital on their recommendation. I remember a millionaire sari merchant who had a prominent shop in Sultan Bazaar getting free treatment declaring his monthly income as Rs. 100 on the recommendation of a senior colleague.

Dr. Dayanand Rao, Professor of Neurosurgery and Dr. Baji, Cardiothoracic surgeon, were doing excellent service with the limited technology available in those times. The normal relationship between a radiologist and a surgeon—one telling another to fix something he has seen—had developed into a personal bond. When not in their operation theatres, both the surgeons would be with me. The time we spent together was highly educative and rich in intellectual content. I learned a lot about stroke in their company.

Stroke is such an ubiquitous term that there is sometimes a little fuzziness about the way it is used. To a physician, a stroke is a deficit in neurologic function resulting from a decrease in blood flow through some specific artery supplying the brain. Further the deficit must last longer than twenty-four hours for the episode to be called a stroke. Anything else is classified as a transient ischemic attack, or TIA. Although TIA clears up within an hour, a few do last somewhat longer before their symptoms disappear.

If all of this has a familiar ring, there is good reason. It is basically the same mechanism by which the heart's deficit is produced when one of its arteries fails to deliver the required volume of blood. It is that universal mechanism of ischemia, the quenching of blood flow and the parching of tissue, that is a common denominator in the killing of cells in so many parts of the body. It carried off Matthew, it carried off my Janatha, and, in one form or another, it will carry off most of us now living. It does its work by suffocating the tissue of its victim. The blood flow stops for much the same reason it does in the coronary arteries of the heart. The build-up of atheroma reaches the critical point when a branch of one of the internal carotid arteries becomes completely occluded. The occlusion may be due to a completion of the atherosclerotic process in that branch itself, or a bit of plaque separating itself from the wall of a larger artery and being propelled as an embolus up into the brain, plugging an already compromised vessel.

The stroke and its attendant ischemia may also be caused by quite another manifestation of this vast syndrome of cerebrovascular disease, namely a haemorrhage into the substance of the brain, which in the elderly is almost always due to long-standing hypertension. Its wall already weakened by long years of abnormally high pressure against it, the fragile atherosclerotic vessel finally gives way at some specific point, resulting in an outrush of blood into the surrounding brain tissue. Such an intracerebral bleed carries a mortality rate of twice the 20 per cent that is usually estimated for occlusive strokes. Haemorrhage accounts for approximately 25 per cent of strokes, and vascular occlusion for the rest.

In takes a great deal of energy to keep the brain's engine functioning efficiently. Almost all of that energy is derived by the tissue's ability to break down glucose into its component parts of carbon dioxide and water, a biochemical process that requires a high level of oxygen. The brain does not have the capacity to keep any glucose in reserve. It depends on a constant and continuous supply being provided by the coursing arterial blood. Obviously, the same is true of oxygen. It takes only a few minutes for the ischemic brain to run out of both before it suffocates. Neurons, the basic nerve cells, are extremely sensitive to ischemia. Irreversible destructive changes begin within fifteen to thirty minutes of the onset of the deprivation. After no more than an hour of the beginning of ischemia, infraction of significant segments of brain tissue becomes inevitable.

The symptoms caused by cell destruction vary, depending upon which vessel is occluded. Although at least half a dozen branches of the internal carotid are particularly susceptible to obstruction, most frequently involved in ischemic stroke is one of the paired middle cerebral arteries. The middle cerebral artery (MCA) supplies blood to most of the lateral surface of the cerebral hemisphere and some of the centres that lie deep beneath the cortex. The MCA feeds the major sensory and motor areas of the cortex—areas that are involved in hand and eye movements, and also the specialised sensory tissue for hearing. It nourishes the region involved in what are called the higher mental functions, such as perception, organised thought, voluntary movement, and the integrated co-ordination of all these abilities. On the dominant side of the brain (the right side for the left-handers and the left for the other 85 per cent of us), the MCA supplies the sensory and motor areas for language. This particular bit of geographic distribution explains why so many stroke victims lose their powers to express and comprehend spoken and written language.

Many strokes are so small that there are few or no immediate, significant symptoms to indicate what has taken place. But with time, such little strokes accumulate, and the evidence of gradual deterioration becomes clear to even the most casual observer. These people, betrayed by their cerebral circulation, take as long to die as they did to grow up. I can never forget an old lady in Pedamuttevi telling me—*dina dina gandam*—death keeps taking little bits of me. Not educated, untouched by science and information, this earthy-wise lady saw that with each attack of dizziness or fainting or confusion she became a little older, a little weaker, and a little more tired. Her steps became more hesitant, her memory less trustworthy, and her interest in life less keen. She knew that for ten years or more, she had been moving step by step towards her eternal rest.

In normal course, I would have been promoted as Professor in 1961, after completing four years of teaching in the Medical College but for the powers-that-be, represented by Major Dr. K.N. Rao, Director Medical Education in the Government, who were still pondering about the credentials of the American education, I had. Finally, Dr. Rao and his enlightened advisers *judged* my American board of radiology that took me three years equated with a nine month post graduate diploma in medical radiology offered by Bombay University held by another colleague, and promoted me as Professor of Radiology in 1962. The disappointment about the delay in getting promotion notwithstanding, the myopic vision of medical bureaucracy and almost the insipid attitude of persons at the helm in comparing a donkey with a horse and declaring both as vertebrates was heartbreaking at the least. Accordingly, I was elevated to the position of Chief Radiologist in the Osmania Hospital.

My children were growing under the watchful eye of Lakshmi and her parents who found in us all their hopes and aspirations. Sabitha was studying in Stanley Girls School, Amita and Sushrut in Vidyaranya School. Later, Sabitha went to Nizam's College for her graduation in Science and we married her off to Madhusudan Rao, a young medical graduate hailing from a place, four miles from Pedamuttevi. I think, I influenced my son-in-law to become a radiologist which took him to England with Sabitha in 1966. Life was moving, as a ship would sail over calm river.

The world goes up and the world goes down,
And the sunshine follows the rain;
And yesterday's sneer and yesterday's frown
Can never come over again.

Towards the end of 1968, Dr. Dayanand Rao, Dr. Baji, Dr. M.V.R. Reddy, a neurologist and I went to England on a three-month Commonwealth Fellowship. I utilised this opportunity to live in Sabitha's home in New Castle upon Tyne, something an Indian father would rarely appreciate.

London is past in the present tense. There are beautiful

buildings and majestic squares everywhere, each with a tale. People so genuinely enjoy posing with the mounted soldiers outside the Horse Guards in Whitehall, stand at the iron gates to Downing Street and crave for a view of No. 10. We watched with awe the Changing of the Guard at Buckingham Palace and peeped into an ongoing debate in the Houses of Parliament. We joined pedestrian crowds enjoying excellent musical performances, from classical trios to flamenco guitar, in the foyers of the Royal National Theatre and adjoining Royal Festival Hall. I saw from South Bank Centre the sunset over the Thames—one of the best sights in London.

We enjoyed the famous English breakfast that can fortify one for a full busy day: bacon, eggs, tomatoes, mushrooms, baked beans, chips, toast, butter, jam and large mugs of tea. Curiosity took us to an Indian restaurant *Rangam.* A Madras curry there was much fiercer than a Madras curry in Madras. The eatery was being run by two misleadingly gentle souls from Kerala.

A friend, took me to London streets with the familiarity of a local. The sight of old clothes, cutlery, tableware, and jewellery being sold at the Brick Lane looked very familiar. There was a Petticoat Lane selling clothing and leatherware. "Saturday is the best time to visit the Portobello Road market in Notting Hill, but you need to be an expert to spot a bargain in the overflow of antiques and bric-a-brac." I also went (he also took me) to Camden Lock, on Regent's Canal in North London, a trendy, eclectic street market on weekends. We used canal boats between Camden Lock and Little Venice, a network of canals and basins near Paddington. After completing our assignment, we decided to tour some other places on our own money. We first went to Paris.

France is the first country that most of my American friends used to associate with Europe, and I had naturally nurtured some formidable stereotypes of the French: non-stop drinkers, womanisers, arrogant. Preconceptions aside, I found the *Francais typqne* neither my fantasised, passionate individualist who exudes *joie de vivre;* nor was he the stiff conformist who disappoints so many first time visitors: he was both. There was explicit rudeness in French people towards tourists. I think the tourists' common *faux pas* is to assume that every one speaks English.

Nobody can be objective about Paris. I was looking for a silver Eiffel Tower and was disappointed to find that it's really rust-red. Steeped in history and allusions right down to its sewers, Paris weaves a spell in stone and sunlight. Palaces and bridges become more than a backdrop: they unite mysteriously with screeching horns and sexy clothes to form a city where nothing falls out of place.

The long boulevards were carved out of the old dark and tangled city of the 1800s in an attempt to foil radicals who could out-manoeuvre the police in little streets and alleys, I was told. I found them attractive as well as practical. The *Arc de Triomphe* on Paris's most celebrated boulevard *Champs-Elysees,* created to celebrate the triumph of Napoleon, was grand and majestic. Paris is laid on both sides of River Seine, a *la* Hyderabad on River Musi. It's an interesting fact that the Left Bank of the Seine refers to the southern area of the city, while the Right Bank refers to the northern half. The Left Bank stands for a more Bohemian life-style, more student-oriented activities and lower costs. Paris has one of the finest subway systems in the world. It's stations are called 'Mo" an abbreviation of the M'etro. Paris boasts of more than 6000 restaurants and an unchallenged reputation as the gourmet mecca of the West. I found many Chinese and Vietnamese restaurants all over the Left Bank.

From here we went to Denmark. Copenhagen, the capital of Denmark, is Scandinavia's largest city but its compactness makes touring easy. We started our visit at *Radhuspladsen,* once the fortified westend of town and now the lively heart of Copenhagen. Next door to Radhuspladsen is the Tivoli Garden, one of Europe's great amusement parks. Tivoli is 20 acres, 110,000 lanterns, and countless ice-cream cones of fun. We wandered into a Hans Christian Andersen wonderland of rides, restaurants, games, marching bands, roulette wheels and pantomimes. There were free concerts, ballet performances, and mime, acrobatic, and puppet shows all around. We took a walk on the Stroget—Copenhagen's trendy pedestrian and shopping district, which stretches through the heart of the old *Koben* (merchants') *havn* (harbour). One could reach the Nyhavn Canal area in 15 minutes, but with stops for street singers and shopping, we took a full afternoon.

Nyhavn, formerly a sleazy sailors' haven, lounges comfortably around the canal. A few smoky taverns and tattoo parlours stubbornly defend their salty turf against a rising tide of chic, expensive cafes. Glamorous sailboats fill the canal. Any historic sloop is welcome to anchor here, temporarily joining the gathering that makes this Copenhagen's ever changing boat pageant.

Just a five-minute walk from Nyhavn is the Amalienborg Palace and Square, official residence of Queen Margrethe II and a good example of ordedy *rococo.* The guards here change with royal fanfare at noon. Beyond the palace, Denmark's Resistance Museum *(Frihedsmuseet)* tells the heroic story of the Danish resistance struggle against the Nazis. The city's most famous (and most photographed) citizen, the Little Mermaid, marked the end of our walk. We then took a cruise through the city's harbour and canals in a boat marked *Netto-Badene.* The excellent National Museum, located in the city centre, traces Danish civilisation from the 2,000-year-old *Gundestrup* Caldron and mummified Viking bodies to trademark modern Danish furniture.

We tasted legendary Danish pastry at one of the *bageriers* found at nearly every corner. Denmark is also popular for open-face sandwiches. Tradition calls for three: a herting sandwich, then meat, and finally cheese, washed down with local beer. We also watched the seagulls, and pedalled a bike into a timeless countryside of windmills, thatched cottages and bluffs facing the sea.

Built on fourteen small islands, Sweden's capital Stockholm has the reputation of being Scandinavia's most beautiful city. The islands—stitched so tightly together by bridges, ferries, tunnels and locks—form such an integral city that visitors need not know on which island they are. Water, fresh or salt, is always within sight, but water does not divide the city, it unites it, giving Stockholm the identity of a 'City by the sea, city of the sea". The great tracts of water add considerably to the city's beauty and give a sense of relaxed serenity. The elegant, monumental architecture set side by side with earthy popular buildings, has a sense of permanence which is somewhat at odds with the reputation Sweden has as a contemporary, forward-looking country.

It was indeed an experience to visit Skansen, the first open-air museum in the world. Skansen is on the island of Djurgarden, which we reached via a short ferry ride. The museum was founded in 1891 by a Swedish teacher, Artur Hazelius, who wanted to show how people had lived and worked in all regions of Sweden, from Lapland in the north to farms in the south. More than 150 historically or culturally important buildings were eventually moved to Skansen's 75 acres of winding roads and rolling countryside. They represent a time span from 1500 to the 1920s-farms, churches, manor houses, belfries and wind-mills. An entire Swedish village of the 1890s has been reassembled, too, complete with a pottery, tannery, glass blower, tinsmith's shop, and the house where Hazelius lived while he was turning his vast dream into reality.

One can see how the rural Swedish live in Skansen—women in bonnets, long dresses, and aprons making their way along rural paths. I could smell wood smoke and hear roosters. Geese and ducks were wandering; pigs grunting. The aroma of baking bread was drifting from an oven. Green moss grew from old thatched roofs. A church bell tolls. A horse munched oats in his stall. A woman shook out a rug. It is a world waking up. Why can't we create a Kakatiya Skasen?

I was very particular to see the building where annual Nobel Prizes are given. We were guided to Stockholm's imposing City Hall, the functioning seat of local government. This graceful creation rises from the water's edge, thrusting into the sky a subtly tapered, 330-foot ltalianate tower, topped with the three golden crowns commemorating Sweden's medieval union with Norway and Denmark. The Golden Hall gets gaspy, *oh-my-God* reactions from awed visitors. At National Art Museum I saw a Rembrandt and other "oppositionist" pictures. From Sweden we went to Russia.

Moscow is all things to all people. It looks European, but its unruly spirit seems closer to Central Asia. To Muscovites, however, Moscow is both a "Mother City" and a "big village", a tumultuous community which possesses an underlying collective instinct that shows itself in times of trouble. Home of one in fifteen Russians, it is huge, surreal and apocalyptic. Its beauty and ugliness are inseparable, its sentimentality emerged out of brutality rooted in centuries of despotism.

Moscow's identity has been imbued with a sense of its own destiny since the fourteenth century, when the principality of *Muscovy* took the lead in the struggle against the Mongols and Tatars who had reduced the Kievan state to ruins. Under Ivan the Great and Ivan the Terrible the "Gatherers of the Russian Lands"—its realm came to encompass everything from the White Sea to the Caspian, while after the fall of Constantinople to the Turks, Moscow assumed Byzantium's suzerainty over the Orthodox world. Despite the changes wrought by Peter the Great—not least the transfer of the capital to St Petersburg—Moscow kept its mystique and bided its time until the Bolsheviks made it the fountainhead of a new creed.

Discounting a couple of satellite towns beyond the outer ring road, Moscow covers an area of about 900 square kilometres! Yet, despite its size and the inhuman scale of many of its buildings and avenues, the general layout is easily grasped—a series of concentric circles and radial lines, emanating from the Kremlin—and the centre is compact enough to explore on foot. Red Square and the Kremlin are the historic nucleus of the city, a magnificent stage for political drama, signifying a great sweep of history that includes Ivan the Terrible, Peter the Great and Stalin. Here we saw Lenin's Mausoleum and St Basil's Cathedral, the famous GUM department store. The Kremlin is surrounded by two quarters defined by ring boulevards built over the original ramparts of medieval times, when Moscow's residential areas were divided into the Beliy Gorod, and the humbler-Zemlyanoy Gorod—both quarters housing a number ot museums and art galleries.

Beyond this historic core, Moscow is too sprawling to explore on foot: you'll need to rely on the metro. To the south-west of the Kremlin, Krasnaya Presnya describes a swathe which includes the White House (the Russian Parliament building); the Novodevichiy Convent further south across the Moskva River; Victory Park, to the south-west; and the Moscow State University, in the Sparrow

Hills. South across the river from the Kremlin, Zamoskvareche is home of the Tretyakov Gallery of Russian art and Gorky Park, while further south are the Donskoy and Danilov monasteries that once stood guard against the Tatars, as well as the romantic ex-royal estate of Kolomenskoe. The main reason to venture out to Moscow's northern suburbs is to visit the VDNKH, a huge Stalinist exhibition park with amazing statues and pavilions, in the vicinity of Moscow's Botanical Gardens and TV Tower.

The underground railway of Moscow was amazing in its size and cleanliness. On huge platforms, busts of communist leaders were kept, making the ambience as that of a museum. The Super Markets were very good, However, I was surprised to find few buyers for neatly kept meat packets. The prosperity meant different in Russia, with hardly one per cent of population buying good food. This was certainly not the communism I learned in Bandar.

From Moscow I proceeded to Tokyo, while Dr. Dayananda Rao and Dr. Reddy returned to India. The restless capital of Japan packed a powerful punch for which I was least prepared. My initial impression was off-putting: ugly buildings are tarred up with eyeball-searing neon and a mess of cables, pavements team with crowds and roads are clogged with traffic. But then I could see behind the barely ordered chaos, remnants of a very different past. Stepping off the main roads I found a world of tranquil back streets, of temples, shrines and wooden houses fronted by neatly clipped bonsai trees.

It's almost impossible to be bored in this city and it was a massive assault on my senses. With money to spend, you can pick up the coolest fashions and eat in fabulous restaurants. But I was also surprised by how affordable things could be. Cheap and cheerful *izakaya* (local bars that serve food) and noodle shacks far outnumber chic French restaurants and high-class *ryotei,* where geishas serve minimalist cuisine, while tickets for a *sumo* tournament or Kabuki play can be bought for the price of a few drinks. The best way to think of Tokyo is not as one city, but as several mini-cities linked by the railway and subway systems. My point of reference was the Yamanote line, a train loop, which connects or encloses virtually everything of interest to the visitor.

Sightseeing destinations outside the loop are mainly within what was once called the Shitamachi, or "Low City", encompassing northeasterly Asakusa and Ryogoku across the Sumida River. At the centre of it all, meanwhile, lies the mysterious green void of the Imperial Palace—home to the emperor and a tangible link to the past.

I found the Japanese very humble and peaceful. Responsibility and accountability towards life was written on their faces. The YMCA, where I was staying, arranged a family tea party for me. I was taken aback by the finesse in their ceremonial way of drinking tea. The concept of family living here was in direct contrast to what I saw in America. In India, though we boast so much about our family-oriented living, lot of buck-passing and parasitic traits go in the name of togetherness in our families. Here, the emphasis was on sharing of effort rather than earnings.

Ruled by the British Empire for nearly 150 years, Hong Kong was the busiest of all the great cities I saw on my tour. Tossed about from one power to another, at the whim of politicians far away it had no great past, but a truly great present. Narrow bazaars with shops filled with a variety of merchandise ranging from electronic gadgets to emerald jewellery and enthusiastic sales persons. Just as an artist depends for his creativity upon the state of his temperament, so the city of Hong Kong, beyond all others, lives by its confidence. It had no natural resources except its people, no cause for its prosperity but its own energy, and it relies upon the readiness of the world to believe in it. Self-assurance amounting almost to chutzpah has been the source of its colossal success in the past, and maintaining a reputation for irrepressible resilience is essential to its survival in the future. Self-esteem is important to this city; chronic self-doubt would be its ruin.

To carry the artistic analogy further, Hong Kong seems to me a true virtuoso among cities, with an inner strength that may ensure its survival. Others may be more profound in their interpretations of life or pursue grander objectives, but none has quite the same dazzling economic techniques. Making money in Hong Kong is like playing concerti anywhere else, and the repertoire of capitalism is exploited here with an incomparable bravado. It is an intensely concentrated, greatly talented, almost obsessively hard-working place, living always on a knife-edge of nerves. I was appalled to see thousands of people living their lives in the boats. It was interesting to see popular balm *Amrutanjan* being manufactured in Hong Kong. I visited the factory. I returned to Bombay after making a brief halt in Bangkok and took the first available flight to Hyderabad. The travel to so many places, exposure to different cultures, prosperity and affluence changed so many things inside me. I must first say to myself what I would be and then do what I have to do. The memories of my struggling youth in the United States came to the forefront of my consciousness. Was it a prophecy?

Heaven is not reached at a single bound,
But we build the ladder by which we rise
From the lowly earth to the vaulted skies,
And we mount to its summit round by round.

I was surprised to find Lakshmi at the Hyderabad airport to receive me with a family friend and a police escort. I was told about the Telengana agitation that had started while I was away and how it turned the peaceful city of Hyderabad into a place of commotion and intrigue. When Lakshmi said, "We are no more safe here", I laughed it away.

For hundreds of years, people from various parts of India made the Telengana region their home. There has never been any instance of intolerance of local people towards them. To the credit of the immigrants, they too adopted the local culture and contributed their own to Telengana culture. Why Andhras should be treated as a different category? They too came and made their home and life in Telengana giving their sweat and blood.

The Andhras are originally an Aryan race, believed to have migrated to the south of the Vindhyas where they mingled with the non-Aryans. The earliest accounts of Andhras date back to Ashoka—the Great Mauryan king (3rd century B.C.)—during whose reign it became an important Buddhist centre. Even today there is good evidence of the early Buddhist influence at Amaravati and Nagarjunakonda, one of the greatest archaeological sites in India.

The Satavahana dynasty (2nd century B.C.- 2nd century A.D), also known as the Andhra, took control of much of central and southern India. They had their capital at Amaravati on River Krishna. They enjoyed extensive international trade with both eastern Asia and Europe. The Satavahanas too were great patrons of Buddhism. Subsequently, the Pallavas from Tamil Nadu, the Chalukyas from Karnataka, and the Cholas all held sway. In the 13th century, the Kakatiyas, with their capital at Warangal, dominated Andhra Desa. They were under constant threat from Muslim incursions.

In 1323, the Tughlak Sultan of Delhi captured the Kakatiya ruler and ended the dynasty. The Tughlaks never cared to annex the Kakatiyan dominions and four local kingdoms arose out of the old Kakatiyan empire. One of these kingdoms was Vijayanagar. The Vijayanagar empire stood as a bulwark against Muslim expansionism for more than 200 years. Vijayanagar had to contend with Muslim sultanates in the north time and again. Sometimes Vijayanagar joined one sultan against another. These tactics finally led to a grand alliance of the sultanates of Ahmadnagar, Bijapur, Golconda and Bidar against Vijayanagar. On January 23, 1565 the Deccan sultans humbled the mighty Vijayanagar army at the battle of Talikota—a defeat of Andhras to the outsiders.

From 1969 to 1972 Andhra Pradesh was rocked by riots, first in Telengana and then in Andhra on the question of bifurcation of the state. One night, our Gurkha guard woke us up to report that miscreants had destroyed our grape garden. The destruction of the garden would have taken at least a few hours. That the guard also colluded with the troublemongers was a very disturbing fact. All this vandalism was done as part of a political agitation.

Receiving threats of sabotage to my clinic in Abids, I decided to stay there and shifted my family from our farm house. My in-laws were rather adamant and decided to stay on the farm and among their labourers. One afternoon, an acquaintance informed me that our farm house was on fire. We rushed to the spot and found the entire place in flames. Almost panicked about the safety of my parents-in-law, I rushed into the burning house. Fortunately, the old couple locked themselves up in the bathroom. The miscreants shouting slogans against Andhras broke open the windows, poured kerosene and threw a torch inside. Having locked the house from outside they presumed the completeness of cremation of our family and left raising victorious slogans. That night was very painful. We returned to Abids house. Frightened and almost broken in spirits, everyone collapsed in the safety of sleep. But there was no sleep in my eyes.

As I briefly mentioned earlier, feeling is controlled by amygdala, a lower, more ancient part of the brain, and thinking by the higher, more recently evolved outer layers. A rudimentary ability to think was superimposed, during evolution, on the pre-existing, genetically programmed behaviour repertoires, each of which probably corresponded to some interior state, perceived as emotion. Fear has to have an emotional tone about it. It has to be unpleasant.

The process of natural selection is a wonderful thing. If the predator's eye-retina-brain combination is geared especially to detect motion, the prey often have, in their repertoire of defences, the tactic of standing frozen, stock-still, for long periods of time. The prey animal may run; play dead; exaggerate its size; erect its hairs and shout; produce foul-smelling or acrid excretions; threaten to counterattack; or try a variety of other, useful survival strategies—all without conscious thought. Only then may it notice an escape route or otherwise bring into play whatever mental agility it possesses.

There are two nearly simultaneous responses: one, the ancient, all-purpose, tried-and-true, but limited and hereditary repertoire; and the other, the brand-new, generally untried intellectual apparatus—which can, however, devise wholly unprecedented solutions to urgent current problems. But the large brains are new. When *the heart* counsels one action and *the head* another, most organisms opt for *the heart.* The ones with the biggest brains more often opt for *head.* In either case, however, there are no guarantees.

Next morning, I wrote to Prof. Harold Jacobson, known as the *backbone* of radiology, requesting him to arrange whatever he could for me to work in the United States. He responded promptly and offered me *a fitting* position in his hospital. I packed up my things and left with Lakshmi and children. This was an action endorsed by both my heart and the head. When I read in childhood about Lord Krishna fleeing to Dwarka to avoid confrontation with Jarasandh who used to frequently attack Mathura, I found his action not befitting a saviour and was baffled about the moral of the story. While taking my family away, I was no more bewildered. Trouble makes life bigger if your attitude toward it is large. Poet Edwin Markham writes:

Defeat may serve as well as victory
To shake the Soul and let the glory out.
When the great oak is straining the wind
The roots sink deeper on the windward side.

□

5

Nations and societies are the people who make them. Those who think that to be a nationalist Indian one must denounce the Western way of living are mistaken. Those who think that following the Western way is the only panacea to succeed are rather more in error. And those others who assert that Western values can make Indian life better are of course the victims of that specific form of want of culture which has its source in the common man's bondage to the present. Anybody who cares to be free from prejudices can free himself from the three mindsets.

I can't stand those cynics for whom there is no country but theirs, no nation like theirs, no kings like theirs, no religion like theirs, no science like theirs. I find them haughty, foolishly vain, self-conceited and stolid. These people fight with words, but they never stake their souls, or body, or their property on what they stand for. On the contrary, their criticism is directed against what they don't have but secretly want to have. The subconscious passivity in these people's mind that their earthworm patience would outlast the strength of *achievers* fills them with sadism—a pathological dreaming about stomping on the heads of the exhausted enemy.

Finding it extremely difficult to forget and forgive my experiences after going back to India, I met Dr. Jacobson with a mixed feeling of repentance and remorse. Discontinuity of fourteen years was too big a reality in the fast-track world of modern medical science. Since I did not have a licence to practise, I joined as a *Fellow*. I took *Flex* examination successfully. Befitting my experience and qualifications, I joined as Associate Adjunct

Radiologist at Montefiore Morrisionia Affiliation in Bronx, New York, with a position of Assistant Professor of Radiology in Albert Einstein College of Medicine there.

There is no place for kindness and compassion in any professional life. You have a skill or you don't have it. I took up my work as a challenge and with a vengeance. I would read till late into night to keep myself abreast of developments in my field. When the question of deciding my sub-speciality came, I opted for ultrasonography but that was preferred also by a young beautiful resident of Dr. Jacobson, Ruth Rosenblatt, who made the right choice. He again made the right choice when I asked for Gastroenterology and his right-hand man in the hospital, Tom Beneventano, also asked for the same. When I gave my choice as Musculoskeletal system, I saw a gleam in his face for he was a giant in his own right in the field of imaging of bones. Was it destiny's script that I work under a professional giant?

Musculoskeletal system is the term used to describe all of the muscles, bones, joints and related structures, such as tendons, ligaments and connective tissue, that function in the movement of the parts and organs of the body. In the clinical assessment of Musculoskeletal system, the patient is questioned about any pain and oedema in muscles, joints and bones, weakness in extremities, limitations in movements and activities, unsteadiness on the feet, fatigability, insomnia (lack of sleep), anorexia (lack of appetite), weight loss and feelings of frustration. The individual's general appearance, age, blood pressure, pulse, respiration, body alignment, ability or inability to move in bed, gait, need for assistance in walking, handgrip, range of motion and internal and external rotation of extremities (arms and legs) are observed.

Further, the presence of contractures (rigidity in joints), deformities, paralysis, contusions (internal injury), lacerations, wounds, foot-drop, wrist-drop, paralysis, allergies, skin rash, or tenderness is noted. Fractures and dislocations are noted and concurrent diseases or conditions investigated include injury to the spinal cord, nerve impairment, cerebrovascular accident, arthritis (inflammatory condition of the joints) and bursitis (inflammatory condition of the tissues surrounding a joint). Also we look for polyneuritis (loss of short term memory and an inability to learn new skills, because of degenerative changes in the thalamus), multiple sclerosis (disseminated demyelination of nerve fibres in the brain and the spinal cord), muscular dystropy (genetically transmitted weakness in skeletal muscles), myasthenia gravis (chronic fatigability and weakness of muscles, especially in the face and the throat), fractures and Meniere's disease and labyrinthitis (both chronic diseases of the inner ear). A family history of carcinoma, diabetes, high blood pressure or tuberculosis rings alarming bells. Laboratory studies important for the assessment are assays of serum and urine for calcium, phosphorus and alkaline phosphtase serum level.

Mainly X-ray films were used to diagnose any abnormality in Musculoskeletal system though biopsies of bone or muscle. Incision and drainage of joints and electromyograms (graphs of electrical activity in the skeletal muscles) were also done occasionally. I was having a very satisfying stint with Dr. Jacobson and gaining deeper clinical insights. As if to cross-check my capabilities I decided to go for the Fellowship of Royal College of Radiology. I wrote the examination in Newfoundland, Canada and travelled to England for the *viva-voice*.

I was staying at YMCA, London. On the night before my examination, Dr. M. Ranga Reddy, Director of Nizam's Orthopaedic Hospital at Hyderabad, knocked my door. It was the last thing that I wanted to happen. Dr. Ranga Reddy was a perfect doctor fit in the bureaucrat mould and was very benevolent in giving unsolicited advice. Even after retirement from the Services, Dr. Reddy used to live as an Army Surgeon and believed himself as highly disciplined. Once, when a radiograph of a distant relative had to be taken, I used my personal money to get the X-ray machine repaired in the Osmania Hospital. Instead of appreciating my action, Dr. Ranga Reddy commented that in my clinic things worked only for relatives and friends. Dr. Ranga Reddy told me that he was also staying at YMCA and saw my name in the lobby and that it was *nice* for him to see me there. Perhaps more inquisitive about who would have sponsored my trip, he asked many penetrating questions. I normally don't lie and never without some good purpose. I thought if I told Dr. Reddy about my exam the next day and somehow failed to get the degree, the entire medical fraternity in Hyderabad would be assured of an exclusive scoop. So, I dexterously fielded his queries without revealing my real mission. I took a big gamble in studying while being a grandfather but to remain a second rate professional. There was no Bharat in America who would hand over the throne to this Rama when he returns after a 14-year exile. I would read some translated heritage books whenever confusion threatened to undermine my determination. One such book was *Yoga Sutras* by Patanjali who lived about 300 years before Christ. Patanjali defined human activities as a five-fold affair. Some are painful and some others pleasurable. They are experience, perversion, delusion, sleep and recollection. Experience comes from perception, inference and evidence. Perversion is an idea of an object, not conforming to its nature. Delusion is an idea conveyed by words, without any reality. Sleep is a condition, which depends on the cessation of perception. Recollection is the calling up of past experience. Patanjali advises control of these activities by practice and detachment. Practice is effort towards concentration. Long, unremitting, sincere practice develops into habit. Success varies according to whether the effort is mild, moderate, or intense. Success is immediate where effort is intense. My biggest recognition came when Dr. Jacobson would introduce himself in medical circles as "my colleague" and say that he works for me.

I used to be very cool and sober like some savant. Dr. Jacobson's secretary, a buoyant American lady with a very expressive body, asked me once how could I be excited. I told her that basically Indians are not very open to their emotions and they particularly guard those that concerned their basic instincts. On the contrary Americans are not so sure about their emotions and they repeatedly have to express them, more as an act of confirmation and validation than communication. So, on every given opportunity they would hold hands, hug each other, kiss, pat, presenting so generously a bounteous feast of gestures and movements for the consumption of others. I only hoped the lady was not indulging in double-*entendre*.

Slowly, stability enveloped our lives. On professional front, I established my credentials and earned the reputation of a Radiology *guru*. I felt the time was ripe for bringing together compatriot radiologists in America and seeking recognition for their calibre which was second to none in the world. We formed Sushrut Society of Radiology comprising radiologists of Indian origin working in America. The society proved very successful in the training and placement of junior radiologists arriving from India. Our efforts also resulted in financial help for the travel of young aspirants coming to America. The feedback from the Society also enriched Indian Radiology in a big way.

I also succeeded in bringing together cultural and social associations formed by Telugu-speaking Indians working in Chicago, San Francisco and New York, under one umbrella organisation—Telugu Association of North America (TANA). A new generation was growing among migrants to America and it was essential to expose them to the heritage and culture of their motherland. In 1977, I was chosen as the Founder President of the Association. We had more than 5000 members, mainly professionals in medicine and engineering. I was elected Chairman of the Board of Trustees for the Hindu Temple Society of North America in New York.

What do religion and culture mean in one's life? Though it does provoke very subjective answers, it is an important question that needs to be examined by those who leave their motherland to live in an alien culture. Each human being is born as something new, something that never existed before. Each is born with the capacity to win at life. Each person has a unique way of seeing, hearing, touching, tasting and thinking. Each has his or her unique potentials, capabilities and limitations. Each can be a significant, thinking, aware, and creative being—a productive person, a winner. Religion and culture provide the ground rules under which a person has to play to be a winner. Inherently, every human being strives for stroking and time structuring. Every person has the need to be touched and recognised by other people, and every person has the need to do something with the time between birth and death. In medical science, we call these biological and psychological needs as hungers. Religious and cultural rituals are the simple and effective ways mankind has evolved to feed these hungers. However, cultures and religions are also not absolutes and they keep changing in time and space. Very often they offer discounting and negative stroking to their people. People who go to live in another country and thereby encounter totally different environment suffer a lot on this account. They must adapt themselves without losing their core uniqueness. It is their success and failure in this that makes all the difference. Many indulge in playing psychological games to get positive strokes, many go into withdrawal to avoid them.

Cultural scripts are the accepted and expected dramatic patterns that are found in every society. They are determined by the spoken and unspoken assumptions believed by a majority of the people. Script themes differ from one culture to another. The script can contain themes of suffering, persecution and hardship (historically, the Jews); it can contain themes of building empires and making conquests (as Romans once did); it can contain themes of snobbery (British), pride (French), or intrigue (Muslims). In America, where people come to escape oppression, to exploit the situation, and to explore the unknown, the basic theme is "struggling into the unknown." In many cases the pioneering and enterprising people acted out this struggle. In India, where people faced the onslaught of invaders, holding onto their land in a stubborn passivity and tiring the invader to return, the basic theme is "holding onto the roots." In many cases population growth and menial living acted out this holding.

What motivates people most to go to America? In my opinion, a majority of people go there to enhance their education and seek better employment opportunities. Most young Indians, on reaching there, get fascinated by American life-style, which is very expressive and flamboyant. Almost all feel the social pressure suddenly off their back, and enjoy the independence inherent in the American way of living. Many young Gujarati ladies would swear by America for liberating them from the clutches of their traditional nagging mothers-in-laws back home. They learn fast the value of money and shed their inhibitions about doing ordinary chores to make the both ends meet. This develops in them dignity of labour, which is unfortunately never seen in India. Indian professionals in America get highly motivated by the appreciation they receive for their performance. Here the appreciation comes directly and spontaneously unlike in India, where it flows through subjective filters of liking and narrow channels of nepotism. A few months' stay in America eventually makes an Indian businesslike. Interestingly, this businesslike attitude fast intrudes into their families and they become vulnerable in life.

We had many young Indian families around us and Lakshmi and I would enjoy observing their chosen American life and their innate Indian mindset. A newly arrived husband would announce to his wife "Honey you've got a letter" and she would say, "Open it". After a few months, she would hate her letters being opened and he would have sleepless nights wondering about their contents.

Indian children who come to America also undergo transformation. In their case it is more real and violent. Amita arrived in America as a studious teenager. She found a resonance in America for her genteel manners, refined tastes and intellectual aloofness. Sushrut came as a shy boy having all the vulnerabilities of his age. Once, a big gathering spent an evening in our house. While taking them round, Lakshmi opened a closet to find Amita sitting and reading inside. We admitted Sushrut in an International School where most Asians would send their children. Sushrut got lured by the American way of living and drawn into a vicious circle of bad friends. Unfortunately, I could not guess it as he used to score good grades in school and was very obedient and meek at home.

After finishing her schooling, I gave Amita the option of going to India for her further education. We came to the understanding that if she were to continue in America she would have to help her mother in household work and had to mend her present self-centred lifestyle. Not all so sure of her offering a helping hand to her mother, Amita decided to go to India. By this time, she had become quite a bit of an American and was apprehensive about the comforts and conveniences that India offered to its people. Judging Delhi closest to her present lifestyle she applied for admission in the upbeat Miranda College and went there.

To her shock, the majority of Punjabi girls in Miranda College exasperated Amita. These girls were much more aggressive than any American girl student. By and large from rich families with enough money to fool around they would virtually pester her into a herd's life. Amita was instantly robbed of her privacy and aloofness she inculcated in America. She, however, persisted there and completed her graduation. She decided to continue in India and applied for a Medical seat in Hyderabad and Kakinada. She failed to get a seat at Hyderabad but got through at Kakinada. She left for Kakinada. In an interesting twist of events, scandal broke out about the leakage of question papers in the entrance exam conducted by Osmania Medical College and a re-exam was conducted. This time she got through, and finally landed herself at the Osmania Medical College. This was in 1974.

I visited Hyderabad to see her settled at college. Many older colleagues and friends expressed their delight at being my daughter's teachers. I had an elated feeling of being a proud father. At TANA, we were inviting prominent Telugu personalities to interact with the Telugus settled there. This was done to maintain cultural continuity and nourish our ethical umbilical cord. I visited N.T. Rama Rao, a prominent icon of Telugu cinema and invited him to visit America. N.T. Rama Rao was one of the most charismatic personalities I have ever met. His command over the language and his way of expressing his thoughts seem to be very much similar to his cinematic roles. With the authority of a King and the grace of a Lord he said in response to my invitation, "Alright we'll see".

In another significant development, computers gave birth to computed tomography, popularly known as CT scanning. The first CT scanner that came into operation in 1972 was meant to study the brain. Using the information provided by an X-ray scanner, a computer constructs cross-sectional images of the tissue under examination. These images, displayed on a TV screen, reveal soft tissues, including tumours, very clearly. These images were particularly valuable as they provided, for the first time, sharp definition of the fluid filled spaces in the brain, medically called as ventricles.

Slowly but surely, with more and more technology inputs enriching it, Radiology has emerged as a major medical speciality that uses beside X-rays, ultrasound, CT and radio-nuclide scanning. The advent of colour Doppler technology gave new meanings to echocardiography. Newer radio-opaque substances when introduced into the body would make organs stand out more clearly under radiation of X-rays and gamma rays. Application of radio-opaque iodine compounds into the kidney, from where they would be excreted into the lower urinary tract, gave new dimensions to intravenous urography. The images that are provided by radio-nuclide scanning started giving insight into the functioning of an organ, particularly the thyroid gland. Terms like arthrograms (X-ray of a joint after injecting a radio-opaque medium), myelograms (X-ray of spinal canal after injecting a radio-opaque medium), and arteriograms (X-ray of an artery after injecting a radio-opaque medium) became commonplace. Recording of moving images started providing information on functions such as blood flow, the movement of the heart walls, urine flow through the kidneys and bile flow through the liver. Soft tissue radiology for breast diseases is done by mammography.

Sushrut completed his schooling in 1977. I asked him whether he wanted to continue college in America or go to India for further education. He gave me the choice. Lakshmi and I decided that he should go to India. Fortunately, he got a seat in Osmania Medical College under Non-resident Indian (NRI) quota through the courtesy of Jalagam Vengal Rao, the then Chief Minister of Andhra Pradesh. He thus became a junior student to his sister. I was happy to see my children going in on medical education. However, my satisfaction proved to be short lived.

Not even a year had passed when I started receiving negative feedback on Sushrut. He was very casual in his studies. He started playing guitar with a music group. Amita completed her MBBS degree in 1979. We married her off to Dr. Maganti Bapineedu, a nephew of Member of Parliament and Congress Party leader from Gudivada. He was appearing for his Masters in Surgery at Andhra Medical College, my *alma mater.* A family friend had arranged the meeting of my daughter and him and they liked each other. At that time I was in New York. They phoned me for my approval and I said "okay". Sushrut was not doing well in Hyderabad. I took him back to America to attempt recuperation of his person-hood. It was a very difficult time and I used to harbour feelings of guilt and depression. One day I was browsing through the *Bhagvad Gita* wherein I came across the 15th verse of Chapter 5, which says:

The lord does not take on
The fault or merit of anyone.
Ignorance veils wisdom,
And misleads people.

The Radiologist in me, so familiar with the anatomy of brain used to feel completely baffled at the diversity of its functioning. I knew that frontal lobes have a special status for the individual's sense of person. A neuroanatomist would say that the frontal lobes constitute the meeting place par excellence for information from the two great functional realms of the brain. The posterior regions, which are involved in the processing of all sensory information, including perception of others, and the limbic systems, where individual motivational and emotional functions are housed, and whence one's internal states are generated, interact here. The frontal cortex turns out to be the realm where neural networks representing the individual's inner *milieu*—his personal feelings, motivations, and subjective knowledge—converge with the system representing the external *milieu*—the sights, sounds, tastes, and mores of the world as transmitted through diverse sensory modalities. Thus, by virtue of their strategic anatomical location and connections, the frontal lobes have the potential to serve as the major integrating station—and this they do.

At the core of personal knowledge, as represented in the brain and particularly in the frontal lobes, there seem to be two kinds of information. One is our ability to know other people—to recognise their faces, their voices, and their persons; to react appropriately to them; to engage in activities with them. The other kind is our sensitivity to our own feelings, our own wants and fears, our own personal histories. Are there pathologies that block the development of knowledge of self and others? I wondered.

One school of psychologists says a person harbours two kinds of contrasts. The first obtains between inside and outside. Inside constitutes the realm of human experience—the flow of subjective feeling which is perceived directly. This phenomenological immediacy with the outside world is contrasted with external actions, movements, postures and speech. We Indians, I feel, strive to achieve the pure and civilised form both in the inner realm, through religious discipline, and in the outer realm, through proper etiquette. The ultimate result is a divided conception of the self, "half ungestured feeling and half unfelt gesture." An inner world of quiet emotion and an outer world of shaped behaviour confront one another as two distinct realms, which we must somehow negotiate successfully within a single body and a single life. Certainly, the tension between the two faces of personal knowledge was directly confronted in Sushrut.

I sought the help of Dr. Jacobson in finding a psychological solution to Sushrut's problem. I had to overcome great inertia in Sushrut to seek professional assistance. Unfortunately the Professor of Psychology at Albert Einstein Medical Centre, in a manner familiar to Westerners, traced Sushrut's behaviour pattern to parental neglect. While it filled me with a deep sense of grief and guilt, it reinforced in Sushrut a defeating justification for his destructive negativism. Is there any fate that cannot be surmounted by scorn? Shakespeare has so nicely summed up life calling it a *web of a mingled yarn*, good and ill woven together.

In January 1983, 1 was invited by the Indian Radiological Association at Bangalore to deliver the keynote address. I used this opportunity to refurbish my knowledge of my roots. The political scene in Andhra Pradesh was getting more and more confused. Regional feelings, caste feelings and factional rivalry were taking their toll on public interest. At TANA we used to discuss the situation with a mix of helplessness and hopelessness. More out of curiosity than anything else, we saw the sudden rise of N.T. Rama Rao, called NTR, on the political scene. The excellent orator in him gave voice to the people watching the politics of intrigue and opportunism practised by puppet politicians. His Telugu Desam concept presented with the authority of some mythological lord demolished the well-built wall of regional division created by vested interests over the years. For a change, the pride of Telugu, overshadowed diminutive regional identities. NTR swept the polls and became Chief Minister in 1983.

Next year, NTR's wife Basava Tarakamma arrived in the United States for treatment of her cancer of the pelvic structures. Under the expert advice of Dr. Nori, who hails from Andhra. NTR was very worried about the cancer and used to ask me many questions about it. I attempted to tell him that cancer seems to arise from the effects of two different kinds of carcinogens. One of these categories comprises agents that damage genes involved in controlling cell proliferation and migration. Cancer arises when a single cell accumulates a number of these mutations, usually over many years, and finally escapes from most restraints on proliferation. The mutations allow the cell and its descendants to develop additional alterations and to accumulate in increasingly large numbers, forming a tumour that consists mostly of these abnormal cells. Another category includes agents that do not damage genes but instead selectively enhance the growth of tumour cells or their precursors. The primary danger of malignancies is that they can metastasize, allowing some of their cells to migrate and thus carry the disease to other parts of the body. Finally, the illness can reach and disrupt one of the body's vital organs. NTR would patiently listen to my Telugu transliteration of these scientific facts and concluded his inquiry with the question whether Basava would be cured? I would always answer in the affirmative knowing fully well that she was suffering from maligant fibrous histiocytoma. She continued treatment under Dr. Nori a well known oncologist.

Being from a place hardly a few miles from Pedamuttevi, Basava Tarakamma stayed with us. NTR would call her every night and spend quite sometime inquiring about her health and how she was feeling in a foreign land. He himself arrived a few weeks later and decided to stay in a hotel. I would joke with Lakshmi about NTR's allegiance and attachment to his wife. He was a very towering personality with a strong faith in himself. He decided to live like a sage and started wearing saffron silk bringing out alive the revered image of Swami Vivekananda.

NTR gave inspiring speeches to Telugu professionals settled in different parts of America. "Come to your land and serve your people", was his usual rhetoric. We could feel the intensity of his conviction about providing good quality of life to his people. However, our seasoning in the businesslike environment of America would restrain us from being carried away by NTR's patriotism. Though nothing dramatic followed his visit, he succeeded in making a very strong impression on the Telugu community in America. His big and erect body, radiating skin and deep voice was the stuff that makes God figures. He had shades of Lord Krishna and Moses rolled into one.

During a medical check-up in America, it was diagnosed that NTR had coronary artery disease. NTR scoffed at all suggestions that he should slow down and look after his health and returned to India. However, before long he had to come back for his heart surgery.

Based on NTR's heart surgery I will attempt to discuss the role of surgical intervention in the management of coronary artery disease. Any surgeon intending to reconstruct blood circulation to the heart would need a road map of the blood vessels and the location of the blockages. The test most frequently used for this information is called a coronary angiogram. In this test, the small blood vessels feeding the heart are imaged with special X-ray techniques. In summary, the coronary arteries are injected with a special dye solution which shows up on X-ray film. As the dye travels down the branches of the coronary artery itself, moving pictures (or angiograms) are taken with the X-ray camera. The entire series of angiographic movies are reviewed by the cardiologist and decisions made about the relative benefits of different treatments.

Surgical reconstruction of the blocked arteries began in the late 1960's and has proven to be remarkably successful. The operation we call Coronary Artery Bypass Grafting (CABG or "cabbage") is the foundation of surgical management. The goal of this operation is to restore blood supply to the heart muscle by creating a new route (hence the word "bypass") for the blood to flow around the blockages.

The first to attempt a direct hook-up to the coronary artery was the famous experimental vascular surgeon, Alexis Carrel. In the early 1900's Dr. Carrel developed most of the techniques for small vessel hook-ups that are still used today. In 1910, Dr. Carrel reported to the American Surgical Association his first attempt to suture a carotid artery graft to the left coronary system in an experimental animal. Although the animal did not survive, the principle of directly grafting into the coronary artery branches was demonstrated. Although this particular contribution went largely unnoticed for over 50 years, Alexis Carrel was eventually honoured for his lifetime accomplishments in developing the techniques of vascular surgery with the Nobel Prize in Medicine.

During the 1930's and 1940's, there were several attempts to bring new blood supply to the heart, most notably the Beck procedure and the Wineberg procedure. However, these procedures did not directly connect a new source of blood to the heart arteries, and the success rates were not very high. In 1940s and early 1950s, the innovative Canadian surgeon Gordon Murray made two major advances. The first was the introduction of the powerful anticoagulant (blood thinner) heparin into the field of vascular surgery. Secondly, Murray reported initial success with direct suturing of a graft to the coronary artery in dogs. However, widespread clinical usage of Murrays discoveries was delayed due to the primitive and largely unavailable angiography techniques present at that time. In 1956, Thal and Demikhov both reported similar success in connecting the internal mammary artery to the coronary artery in experimental animals.

The development of modern surgical techniques awaited major developments in X-ray diagnostic techniques. It was Dr. Mason Sones at the Cleveland Clinic who accidentally injected the angiography dye into the mouth of the coronary arteries for the first time in a living patient. Aware of the significance of this observation, Dr. Sones went about designing catheters and techniques to routinely X-ray the various coronary arteries in human patients. The utility of the Sones (and later) techniques for safely documenting coronary artery blockages in humans was readily apparent and the procedure gained immediate popularity throughout the world.

Meanwhile, other researchers were pursuing a means of supporting the circulation while the heart beat was temporarily stopped. Using mechanical devices to pump the blood and restore the oxygen content of the blood, the artificial heart-lung machine was gradually designed and modified in the 1950's and early 1960's. At first, the heart-lung machine was used by surgeons to correct congenital anomalies of the heart, such as birth defects seen in "blue babies". However, as improvements were made in heart-lung technology, its use spread to other types of heart operations. Although most of the initial cases of coronary artery surgery took place on the beating heart without the benefit of the heart-lung machine, surgeons quickly saw the advantages of performing these reconstructions when the heart was motionless.

Coronary Artery Bypass Grafting doesn't remove the obstructing blockages in the arteries. The procedure "reroutes" the flow of blood by using a "detour" pathway. Typically, the blockages occur in the first centimetre or two of the major branches feeding the heart. The smaller branches are usually not involved until very late in life. Thus, it is possible to hook a new source of blood into the artery just beyond the last major blockage. Blood flows into the artery through a different path (such as a vein bypass graft) and reaches the heart muscle tissue where it is needed. The heart doesn't care how the blood gets there, as long as it gets what it needs during times of peak demand. Once the volume and pressure of blood flow is restored, the symptoms of exertional chest discomfort are relieved. The most common material used to build this new pathway is a vein from the lower extremity. In each of us, there is a long straight vein called the Greater Saphenous Vein (or GSV) running from just inside the ankle bone up to the groin. This vein is just one of a large series of veins in the lower extremity. However, the GSV is the right size, shape, and length for use as a bypass conduit. The other major vessel used as a bypass graft is the Left Internal Mammary Artery (LIMA). Recent studies have shown that the LIMA is more resistant to atherosclerotic deposition than even the native coronary arteries. This vessel courses alongside the undersurface of the breastbone (sternum). By detaching the lower end of the LIMA, the vessel can be transplanted to the surface of the heart.

Regardless of which conduit is used for the bypass, the main advantage offered by this surgical approach is the restoration of blood supply to the heart. The vein or mammary artery provides a new and unobstructed route for blood flow. When the surgeon connects the bypass to the native coronary artery beyond the obstruction, blood has a new path in which to flow into the blood vessel beyond the blockage. Then when the heart demands more blood flow, the situation can be met by the new source of blood flowing through the bypass graft. It is important for the surgeon to provide a bypass for each major branch that is obstructed. In that way, the whole heart will have more blood supply, and the anginal (chest) pains will be relieved.

A typical CABG operation begins with a vertical opening into the front of the chest. The breastbone (sternum) is divided with a specialised (reciprocating) saw, similar to a "jig" saw used in woodworking (only designed just for this incision). The split sternum is spread open with a device that functions like a winch. The soft tissues in front of the heart are parted, and the membrane surrounding the heart (the pericardium) is incised. Next, the surgeon removes the Internal Mammary Artery from the chest wall to provide a donor artery for grafting.

Simultaneously, an assistant surgeon proceeds with harvesting additional conduit, usually the Greater Saphenous Vein (GSV) from the inside of the calf or thigh. This vein is long, straight, and of the proper caliber for use as a donor graft to the heart. In the average patient, there is ample length to reach all the potential target vessels of the heart. In addition, the leg contains many redundant veins, so removal of the GSV does not impair the return of blue blood from the extremity.

After all the donor vessels are harvested, the patient's blood is thinned with a large dose of the potent anticoagulant heparin. This renders the blood incapable of clotting when exposed to the plastic tubing and surfaces of the heart-lung machine. The patient's circulation is connected to the heart-lung bypass circuit, and the body placed onto the support machinery. Then the body temperature is lowered (by refrigerating the blood as it circulates through the machine). In addition, blood flow to the heart is separated from that going to the rest of the body by a vascular clamp applied to the aorta just below the insertion of the arterial return cannula. The coronary arteries are then perfused with a cold potassium solution. The heart is immediately rendered motionless, cold, and relaxed. The body is preserved by the nutrient flow provided by the heart-lung circuit, while the heart is preserved by the low temperature and other conditions managed by the surgeon.

Next, each target vessel is identified as it runs across the surface of the heart. For each intended bypass, the surgeon makes a tiny opening into the front wall of the target coronary artery with a very fine knife. The opening is expanded with specialized scissors. A donor vessel, either vein or IMA is stitched to this opening with delicate fine suture material. Currently, the best suture material is made from polypropylene and is finer in diametre than human hair. After all the grafts are sutured to the heart arteries, the vascular clamp is released, allowing blood to flow into the native heart arteries again. For the IMA, it is already connected to the native circulation proximally, so it can immediately begin its job of perfusing the heart.

Internal Mammary Artery Grafts are already attached at their origin from the main artery to the arm (the subclavian artery). Blood flowing through the IMA directly comes from the subclavian artery. However, GSV grafts are detached at both ends. After connecting one end of the vein to the coronary artery, the other end must then be connected to a source of red blood. This is done by partially occluding a segment of the ascending aorta with a specialized, curved vascular clamp. Holes are created in the front wall of the aorta, and the veins are anchored to these openings with fine suture. After releasing this partially occluding clamp, the veins fill with red blood from the aorta and deliver this blood to the coronary arteries downstream.

After the heart has had a chance to recover from the temporary arrest period, the heart-lung circuit can be gradually withdrawn. When the heart is beating strongly again, then the heart-lung machine is stopped, and the equipment removed. The anticoagulant (heparin) is chemically reversed (with a drug called prolamine). The surgeon then inspects and controls any remaining bleeding. Finally, the wounds are closed and the patient sent to Intensive Care for recovery.

The average patient, without any major post-operative problems, can leave the hospital in about 6 days from surgery. It will take about another two to three weeks for most patients to feel strong and regain normal body habits, such as appetite, sleep patterns and bowel patterns. For patients who work in non-physical jobs, many can return to employment within 4 to 6 weeks of surgery. Some patients return to work even earlier, depending on their level of energy. Usually, antianginal medications are no longer needed. However, high blood pressure and diabetic medications will often continue as they did pre-operatively. After full recovery, the vast majority of patients (over 90%) can return to full and active lifestyle, including exercise, travel, and employment.

A big troupe of officials and local doctors accompanied NTR. I took special notice of the tall, lean young cardiologist from Nizam's Orthopaedic and Specialities Hospital, Dr. B. Soma Raju, who would always be by NTR's side with the alertness of a doctor and the affection of a disciple. NTR was admitted to the Texas Medical Centre at Houston. Legendary cardiac surgeon Dr. Coley performed the surgery. His Indian colleague Dr. Mathur assisted him. NTR responded well and recovered faster than any other younger patient. There was an amazing inner strength in him.

The Texas Medical Centre started with a dream to create a facility, where people from all walks of life could have access to the best healthcare anywhere—whether they were rich, poor, famous, alone, young, or old. In more than 50 years since that dream originated, it had been realised many times over. On any given day, one could find people from every social circumstance and many of the world's nations seeking treatment at the centre's renowned institutions. In the Texas Medical Centre, there had always been something to meet everybody's needs. The county's two trauma facilities were located in the centre, as were institutions specialising in every imaginable aspect of healthcare, including care for children, cancer patients, heart care, organ transplantation, terminal illness, mental health, and wellness and prevention.

There were more than 30 (now 42) institutions run on non-profit basis, and dedicated to the highest standards of patient and preventive care, research, education, and local, national, and international community's well-being. These institutions included hospitals and two speciality institutions, two medical schools, four nursing schools, and schools of dentistry, public health, pharmacy, and virtually all health-related careers. It was where one of the first, and still the largest, air emergency service was created; a very successful inter-institutional transplant program was developed; and more heart surgeries were performed here than anywhere else in the world.

I took a trip to China, during this period as Deputy Leader of a group of Radiologists from America under a people-to-people programme. The whole world has always been fascinated by China because China is so strange. Everything is different here—the food, the clothing, the language, the music, the architecture—whatever you name is exotic, sometimes downright odd. Even the alphabet: I couldn't even guess the street signs, much less read them. To me, all the letters looked like melted television antennas. Beyond this sense of complete otherness, I also found China fascinating because it was the big dragon, India's perceived enemy.

I must confess that I was wrong on many counts. Beijing, with a population of over a million, has a relatively low crime rate. Petty theft more than any other crime seems to affect people here. This usually occurs in crowded areas, restaurants, public transport stations and near hotels. I visited Tian'anmen Square, now more known for the massacre that took place here during a public demonstration for democracy. It is a real huge place. I saw there Chairman Mao Memorial where an overwhelming sense of awe, with Chinese tourists come to pay homage to Mao's embalmed corpse. There are also Imperial palaces, called the Forbidden City, a vast complex of palaces and gardens. This city within a city was the home to China's emperors for five centuries.

The brash modernity of Beijing came to me as a surprise. Traversed by freeways and spiked with high-rises, this vivid metropolis was China at its most dynamic. For the last thousand years, the drama of China's imperial history was played out here, with the emperor sitting enthroned at the centre of the Chinese universe. The dynasty perished but it remained spiritually and politically the heart of the country. Between the swathes of concrete and glass, I found some of the finest temples and the grandest remnants of the Imperial age.

While convalescing after the surgery, NTR observed that most of the Indian doctors in America, a majority of them from his own State, were holding good positions and regarded as among the best in their fields. He then concluded that if proper facilities were provided back home, these doctors should have no problem in returning and serving their own people. Before, returning to India, he toured different places and shared his thoughts with a large number of doctors in different cities. Almost, everywhere, to his surprise, he was asked to discuss the matter with me.

We shared NTR's vision of promoting the highest quality health status for all people by networking existing institutions with a super-speciality centre of international standards. I was a bit apprehensive though. NTR ridiculed me for keeping the bad dream alive for so long and almost ordered me to return. I have agreed to set and achieve individual and collective goals of the highest possible standards of patient and preventive care, of research and education, and of local, state and national community's well-being and a dream was born.

The clod, the marble, and the gold
are one in his hands;
Whose equal heart holds the same gentleness
lovely and unlovely things, firm set.

In 1985, I completed 60 years of my life. Traditionally, this occasion is celebrated as *shashtipurthy* to take stock of one's achievements and for thanksgiving. The family and friends organised a big function to facilitate Lakshmi and me. I announced my idea of starting an old age home for Indians who come here as parents either following their upcoming sons or become old struggling their lives to settle their children in America. In most of the cases they end up as unwanted burden. However, this could not be done. NTR sent Dr. M.S.S. Koteswara Rao and Dr. M. Venkat Rao to negotiate with me the modalities of setting up a super speciality hospital in Hyderabad, meeting international standards. TANA members collected $ 100,000 for this purpose. We were offered land on the outskirts, which we declined. We preferred Chiran Palace as the location for the hospital. That was not agreed to. Instead, NTR decided to convert Nizam's Hospital into a super speciality hospital with research and teaching facilities and the Nizam's Institute of Medical Sciences (NIMS) was born. I joined as the first Director of the Institute on December 2, 1985.

I was offered a decent salary suitable to the post of Director which I refused and preferred to work on honorary basis. Some well wishers advised me to take the salary offered and if I intended could give as donation to poor patients. I have been a poor economic student and a poor accountant. I did not want to have any hassles with accounts keeping and dealing with income tax people. Hence I promised that I work for no salary. My wife and children were extremely pleased with my decision. My motto has been a quotation of Stephen Grellet.

"I shall pass through this world but once
Any good thing therefore That I can do
Or any kindness That I can show
To any fellow creature.
Let me do it now.
Let me not defer nor neglect it
For I shall not pass through this way again."

□

6

Not many, particularly within the system, took kindly to the idea of converting a well established and traditionally run hospital into a super speciality centre of some hypothetical and futuristic excellence. I met NTR and informed him about the almost omnipresent indifference in his government about his dream institute. He gave me an inspiring lecture on the virtue of perseverance and convinced me to hold on. I, in turn, convinced him to give me a small break so that I could visit Lakshmi in the United States. In fact, by seeing the bandicoot mentality, passivity and inertia against change, I made up my mind to get all the positive forces together and liberate the state healthcare machinery from the clutches of vested interests and ghettos of petty minds. Many doctors were enjoying almost unaccountable but highly privileged positions. The bureaucrats would expect pampering for doing the minimal work they were handsomely paid for. I had made up my mind to stay on and stage a fight-back. By profession, doctors fight against everything that troubles the health of their patients. What an opportunity I had on my hands to take on this fight, to the newer domain of greed and rapacity, I told myself.

I was entering the airport lounge for security check when a messenger came running from the Secretariat with a sealed cover. With a blank mind I opened the envelope. It contained the Government Order converting the Nizam's Hospital into the Nizam's Institute of Medical Sciences. It was 24th day of March 1986. When the aircraft flew minutes later, it was a real takeoff.

When I announced my decision to resign, almost no one at the Albert Einstein College was convinced about my action. Some reminded me about the experiences I had had in 1970's, some others told me about the plight of a new generation of Indian Radiologists in America who looked to me for guidance. A Professor of Rheumatology and Metabolism went to the extent of describing India as a land of floods and famine and offered me a bet on my "inevitable" return within a year. I heard them all but stuck to my plans. Many colleagues were sad and many others were angry. My residents almost cried. But one has to free oneself from bondage to pursue higher goals. Nothing comes without its counterbalance. To get something you have to forego something else. You can't fill a vessel with anything till you empty it first. When I landed back in Hyderabad on April 16 with Lakshmi, I was fully empty and thus receptive to anything that would pour in.

We decided to build the Nizam's Institute of Medical Sciences, (acronym NIMS) on the lines of the All India Institute of Medical Sciences (AIIMS) at Delhi, a centre of excellence in healthcare under the Government umbrella. We invited all doctors working in the hospital to join the Institute under service conditions that lay stress on academic activities and research besides clinical work. Consequently, the doctors would be forbidden from doing private practice and put in extended working hours in the hospital. Many joined, many left, both equally welcomed. Few, like Dr. Raja Reddy, a renowned neurosurgeon remained in the Institute without opting for either. The local Member of the Legislative Assembly P. Janardana Reddy and former Chief Minister of Andhra Pradesh J. Vengal Rao were my most vocal critics. However, I will be unfair to these leaders in presuming that they were harbouring any personal ill feelings against me. In public life you end up holding on to positions and taking sides. Had not even a man as judicious and as principled as Bhishma end up fighting Pandavas?

For more than a year intense efforts were made to roll back the Institute into its earlier form. Funds promised to transform the hospital into an Institute didn't arrive casting a long spell of frustration. When I approached the Government for funds to buy a CT scan, a senior bureaucrat reminded me of my stature in Radiology and grinned in black humour saying, "Had we had money to buy these things why would we invite you here?" In fact, it was a hopeless situation where funds were not available to provide even basic facilities like fans and toilets, leave alone procurement of equipment. Though permission from the Government to charge money from those patients who could afford to pay was available from as back as 1980, nothing was done to generate any revenues by the hospital authorities. When the Institute started functioning, patients were not accustomed to paying for the treatment they received. I considered it fit that before we started collecting charges from patients, an awareness about the changed set-up and the need for payment was created. A three-member committee comprising Dr. K. Venugopal Naidu, Dr. Balaparameshwar Rao and Dr. Veeraraghava Reddy, all former Superintendents, was constituted to decide tariffs. Meanwhile, we levied a very moderate fee of Rs. 5 for every new outpatient registration. This was described as a disaster for the poor. We had 246 beds. From the Rs. 1.22 crore grant available from the Government, about a crore of Rupees was going towards salaries. We very urgently needed, import of sophisticated equipment worth Rs. 6 crore to provide speciality treatment. It was foolish on the part of anybody to imagine that anyone could run a super speciality hospital without collecting at least fair charges for the treatment given. However, many learned men of that time preferred to be blind to the logic that there was no harm in making rich patients subsidise the cost of treating the poor.

Good support came from Health Minister Dr. Daggupati Venkateswara Rao. The Government decided to give Rs. 4.5 crore over three years. The first disbursement of Rs. 1 crore helped us in augmenting Cardiac Catheterisation Lab. Besides adding newer equipment, I laid special emphasis on creating paying rooms for patients who could afford to pay.

During this period Dr. Pratap C. Reddy decided to start his second Apollo Hospital in Hyderabad. Big hype was created around him and his hospital at Madras and other business ventures.

Notwithstanding Apollo's aggression and drive, NIMS became the first hospital in the country to perform a balloon angioplasty. The feat was achieved by Dr. B. Soma Raju. The Cardiology Department flourished due to the hard work put in by Dr. A.

Rajagopala Raju and Dr. B. Soma Raju. In September, 1987, under a collaborative programme with Wayne State University Prof. Joshua Wayne performed valvuloplasty replacing the risky cardiothoracic surgery. The word spread, "If you have a chest pain, rush to NIMS". In 1987, NIMS conducted 10 medical education programmes when 56 visiting professors shared their expertise with local doctors. A Nuclear Medicine Department was set up to reinforce the initial lead taken by NIMS doctors in this important area of medicine. On March 25, 1988, we commissioned Gamma Camera.

I had brought with me a big collection of radiographs from Albert Einstein College and used to discuss them with my colleagues. There are no *ifs* and *buts* or *may be* and *perhaps* in Radiology. Either you see something or you don't see. When most patients seek a doctor for a medical diagnosis, they generally assume that the process will clearly and directly reveal the truth about their condition. Their assumption is that the diagnostic procedure will reveal their illness in much the same way that cutting open an apple bears its core. In most cases, however, nothing could be farther from the truth. In medical diagnosis doctors often begin with their personal biases. Physicians obtain a limited set of information from tests and/or other techniques. Through this analysis based on personal understanding, experience and awareness, doctors attempt to comprehend the truth of the condition. There are few who end up treating lab reports instead of their patients.

I still recall telling my colleagues a metaphor during one of my morning *discourses* in the Radiology Department. The metaphor referred to the stages of development of the Radiologist. At the first level he is likened to a person standing on a mountaintop. He is unable to perceive what is on the top of the opposite peak. At the next level the student can see that something is there. At a higher level the student can perceive that someone is standing on the opposite peak but he or she still lacks the ability to perceive anything about that person. At many succeeding levels, more and more can be perceived about this person until, ultimately, at the most advanced degree of ability, the student recognises precisely who is there.

The Andhra Pradesh Legislative Assembly passed the NIMS Bill 1989 on March 31, 1989, the last working day of the Budget session, conferring on NIMS the status of a university. The Speaker of the Assembly G. Narayana Rao took special interest in tabling the Bill. Piloted by Dr. Daggupati Venketswara Rao, Minister for Medical Education and Health, the Bill sought to promote excellence in medical care, improve research facilities and award degrees and diplomas to students. The Bill was debated for nearly two hours. Although NTR accepted many amendments to the Bill suggested by the Opposition, particularly by a Marxist Legislator. Opposition members belonging to Congress, Communist Party and Majlis walked out protesting against it. Many of these members, very well known to me, while trooping out looked at me sitting in the visitors' gallery and tossed those typical political smiles that are more mysterious than that of Monalisa. The Bill later got the assent of the Andhra Pradesh Governor Kumudben Joshi and NIMS became a University in June, 1989.

In the Assembly Elections held in December 1989, NTR's Telugu Desam Party was defeated by the Congress and Dr. Marri Channa Reddy became the Chief Minister of Andhra Pradesh. As per the NIMS Act, he also became Chairman of it's Governing Council. In February, 1990 he came to NIMS to see a patient. While Dr. Soma Raju and I were escorting him back to his car he inquired, almost jokingly, about the trim physique of Dr. Soma Raju. I informed Dr. Channa Reddy about the regularity of Dr. Soma Raju in playing tennis. Extending his good mood he wondered how could Dr. Soma Raju steal time to play tennis from the watchful eye of a taskmaster like me. Almost as if putting his seal of approval on his observations during the visit, Dr. Channa Reddy quipped while getting into his car, "Even out of power, I was appreciating the progress of the Institute."

After a couple of months, Dr. Channa Reddy left for the United States for his kidney transplant. He expected the Telugus living there to repeat the reception they gave to NTR during his earlier visits. In fact, Dr. Channa Reddy did get the most suitable and respectful response from Telugus there and the TANA looked after him very well. However, the spontaneity that NTR evoked in Telugus living in America was absent this time. Some friends of Dr. Channa Reddy showed him video films about NTR's American visits. The images of his political foe being received as a God and his charisma swaying crowds perhaps added anguish to the ailing man. Notwithstanding the fact that his companions almost irritated TANA office-bearers by nagging for donations to the Chief Minister's Cyclone Relief Fund, Dr. Channa Reddy thought it wise to hold me responsible for all that NTR got and he did not. He started sending fax messages to his Secretariat inquiring about happenings in NIMS and went to the extent of convening a Governing Council Meeting of NIMS even before he landed back in India. Principal Secretary G. Kumarswamy Reddy, an outspoken official, gave signals to me that a conspiracy had already been hatched to get me out of the Institute. The meeting took place on July 31, 1990. Dr. Channa Reddy started by giving himself the credit for mooting the idea of this Institute in 1978 itself and that the NIMS was not even the least of what he dreamt it to be. He lost no opportunity in criticising every thing that I had done and even the best of the achievements were trivialised. He even chided me for collecting a *mere* Rs. 1 crore as donations saying that with so many rich friends in the United States I should have collected that much every month.

I listened to the Chair with utmost calm and without refuting anything Dr. Channa Reddy chose to say. After the meeting ended, I sought an appointment with him on the very next day. I was asked to come at 5 PM to his house. Though I reached there on the dot, I was not given an audience. Visitors coming after me were sent in, as I waited outside his room. At 8.50 PM Dr. Channa Reddy finally called me in. He gave me a grimy look and started volleying incoherent charges including that I promoted incompetent doctors and recruited staff on caste lines and purchased useless pieces of equipment that were rusting with suppliers for want of buyers. He didn't allow me to say anything. Taken aback by his prejudice and arrogance, I told him that I didn't mind going out of NIMS but the Institute, functioning so well and growing energetically, should not be disturbed. This was the least that Dr. Channa Reddy expected from me. He threw up his arms in a fit of rage and asked me how I dared to talk in that manner to him. He was the Chief Minister and I was a mere government servant. I got up from my chair and bade him good night. It all took less than 10 minutes. In that longest night of my life I recalled a poem I learned in Bander:

The mountain and the squirrel
Had a quarrel
And the former called the latter 'little Prig'.
Bun replied,
'You are doubtless very big;
If I'm not so large as you,
You are not so small as I.
Talents differ: all is well and wisely put;
If I cannot carry forests on my back,
Neither can you crack a nut.'

The next day when I put in my resignation letter it sent a shock wave among the faculty and staff of the Institute. Many senior faculty members gathered in my office. I almost surprised them by being calm and composed. There was no anxiety, bitterness, or even customary dejection that one normally acquires at the time of giving up or giving away. I was absolutely clear in my mind that I was not giving up and not giving away. The Chair of the Director was not something to which I should have been possessive about at that point of my career. Having had the best in my profession in terms of money, position and freedom, I had no fun in doing something that led to acerbity. With NTR, the creator of the Institute himself in wilderness, there was nothing much I could have done to salvage the situation.

I made my exit very unceremonious, brief and surgical. I bundled my personal papers, loaded them into my car, which was parked near the Radiology Department, and drove back to my house. Lakshmi saw to it that I remained at ease at home after *losing* my job. After a long time, I was sitting with her without anything to pursue in particular. Though my wife liked spending a lot of time with me at home, she saw unrest in me since she knew in her heart of hearts that my objective is different.

The staff at NIMS went on strike protesting against my

politically engineered exit. Dr. Soma Raju and other senior physicians offered to quit in solidarity against political interference in the Institute. I had to go to NIMS to pacify tempers and virtually pleaded with the hurt employees to go back to their work.

To me, there were three options. Go back to the United States and pass into history as a Radiology *Guru,* join some other hospital and enrich Radiology in the country by training young doctors (there was an offer from Jaslok Hospital in Bombay) or set up my own clinic and start seeing patients who had always been my primary passion. The idea of retiring never occurred to me because I always feel that one retires only while joining death.

My good friend K.S. Rao had started Medwin Hospital sometime back. He would consult me regularly on matters both personal and professional. He wanted me to be on the lookout for a suitable groom for his daughter, someone of the like of Dr. Soma Raju. I suggested Dr. Ramesh who was doing fellowship under Dr. Soma Raju. After marriage, Dr. Ramesh, who used to be very studious and most of the time withdrawn into his own world underwent a metamorphosis under the watchful eye of his father-in-law and became the chief executive of Medwin Hospital.

The father-in-law-son-in-law duo not only added a fourth option to my list but also succeeded in making me close on that. I was grounded as Chairman of the Medwin Hospitals. Though insignificant by any yardstick of professional excellence, this position gave me some of the biggest lessons in advanced technology healthcare delivery in a developing country without muddling by the State. The NIMS had successfully brought in advanced healthcare technology within the affordability of a large section of the population. But this was done with the support of the State. The Government gave money to buy equipment and provided assistance in many different forms. There was, however, much more to healthcare delivery than purchase of latest equipment or construction of immaculate rooms and amenities. Sitting in the office of Chairman of a privately owned hospital where everything was created, run and maintained on commercial terms, was a new experience for me.

The United States of America is seen as an epitome of

commercialisation. You are paid by the hour to even talk to and have to pay for the advice you seek. Even the best of friends share the bill for the meal they eat together. It sounds too mean and selfish in this part of the world where one is judged by the doles one distributes and the sacrifices one makes for others. But then, what is hidden to the external world is an inherent honesty in the American way of living. What is selfishness? Is there anything wrong in being selfish? The plenty of time available at the Medwin Hospital and a change from the chaos and crowd of the big to the equipoise and serenity of the small helped me contemplate and learn some good lessons. We formed the Centre for Health & Allied Research in Medicine at the Medwin to undertake academic work that I always considered imperative for any professional, particularly physicians.

The internal strife in the Congress Party led to the exit of Dr. Channa Reddy as Chief Minister. N Janardana Reddy took over as the new Chief Minister and thus became the chairman of NIMS Governing Council. In a gesture placed somewhere between goodwill and reconciliation, Janardana Reddy invited me to the Annual Function of the Institute. He requested me to assist him in shaping up the Super Speciality Institute coming up at Tirupati. In a path-breaking move, Janardana Reddy appointed me Chairman of the Governing Council of the Sri Venkateswara Institute of Medical Sciences (SVIMS).

This move was met with stubborn silence in the Secretariat. Although I functioned for over two years in the capacity of Chairman and led efforts in starting the Institute, I received no formal orders to that effect from the Government. Meanwhile veteran Congress leader Kotla Vijay Bhaskara Reddy replaced Janardana Reddy. The new Chief Minister didn't like the idea of a Physician sitting as Chairman in the Governing Council of a State-supported Institute. During my brief absence while on a visit to the United States, he made himself the Chairman. The *babus* in the Secretariat patted themselves on their backs for ensuring all these days that no formal appointment order had been issued saving them the trouble of issuing a sacking order.

NTR swept the polls. NTR asked me to take over the reins of

NIMS, which I respectfully declined as I hated political interference in the functioning of professional institutions. NTR, however, made me agree to be the Advisor to the Government for Medical Health Services, with a rank of State Cabinet Minister.

A cascade of events saw most of the members of the Telugu Desam Legislature Party chose N. Chandra Babu Naidu, a young leader married to NTR's daughter, as their leader making him the Chief Minister. NTR passed away in the early hours of January 18, 1996.

The demise of the tallest personality in the contemporary Telugu history left a trail of confusion and chaos. Chandra Babu Naidu saw it all with great maturity and handled things with finesse and intelligence. Carrying on the legacy of NTR in true earnest, he invited me to chair a committee of twelve eminent doctors on healthcare reforms in the State. I was also invited to join as a member of the State Planning Commission.

Among many reforms that the committee recommended the most important one was grant of autonomy to Government Hospitals. We proposed the setting up of Hospital Development Societies with Superintendents as chairpersons. The society, including members of the local community, would make the hospital a matter of pride for the town. It should have freedom to raise funds locally through contributions and also from user charges. Freedom to fix the quantum of user charges should be left to the society and a minimum of 75% of the revenues should be retained at the hospital itself. We also proposed a code of conduct for doctors. We all feel proud of talking about our democratic traditions but the way we run our healthcare system would make our erstwhile colonial masters blush.

Gradually, NIMS started loosing its sheen. Frequent strikes, confrontation among various cadres, lack of focus and short-term management strategies almost brought the Institute on to the verge of degeneration. Lacking vision and any long-term commitment the administration had turned itself into a fire-fighting brigade. After Prof. I. Dinakar completed his term as Director in September 1996, for many months the Institute was managed in an ad-hoc manner. First, Dr. K. Eswara Prasads Rao, Director, Medical

Education in the State Government, took additional charge and then on his retirement in January 1997, V.S. Bhaskar, Joint Secretary to the Government, became in-charge Director. The Governing Council invited me to find a good leader to put the Institute back on rails. Many renowned physicians were sounded but they backed out for reasons ranging from scepticism about additional investment in infrastructure to perceived political interference. Someone from within NIMS was not acceptable to the Chief Minister. After an impasse of many months, I volunteered my services to take over the leadership and restore order. Under the pressure of Dr. N. Janardan Reddy the then Minister of Health, Medicine & family Welfare. It was a difficult decision on my part. The bitterness of 1989 was still there. What would I gain by fighting a cascade of negative forces and what would I achieve? Preferring commitment to pride and prejudice, I rejoined NIMS as Director on May 9, 1997. An old grateful patient sent me a congratulatory note citing Psalms 55:22 from the Holy Bible:

Cast thy burden upon the Lord,
and he shall sustain thee:
He shall never suffer the righteous to be moved.

There were three categories of doctors embodying the Institute: (1) those who can't get an equivalent job anywhere else, (2) those who hold on to see an administrative office coming, and (3) those who have grown up giving all they had for the Institute. I find the first group wondering at the way Institute was going with an astonishing passivity and inaction. The second group was watching the developments taking a detached emotional position. The smallest third group was restless and anxious to make things turn towards good. I will never forget the support I received from Prof. S. Manimala Rao, Anaesthetist and a very able administrator, Prof. V. Subbalakshmi Murthy, Radiologist and a gracious leader, Prof. V. Shantaram, internist and an excellent teacher, Prof. S. Venkataratam, Radiation Oncologist and very rational, and Dr. Pinjala Ramakrishna, Vascular Surgeon and very enthusiastic about setting the things right. My professional stature proved too heavy in rolling flat the ambitions of many aspiring young Directors. The positive attitude of the Chief Minister proved very crucial in curbing a parasitic mentality that had seeped into the Institute through bureaucratic interference.

With Institute back on rails, I started looking into the larger problems of managed healthcare. The technological gains made by the nation need to percolate to the grassroot level of our society leading to enhancement of the basic quality of life. One of the major achievements of the Indian health services system over the last fifty years has been the development of an extensive institutional network in the public sector. This network, despite severe limitations in the delivery of preventive, promotive and rehabilitative healthcare, served as an institutional life support system for the poor in the country. However, the profound infusion of technology in healthcare undermined the approach to primary healthcare and enforced an entirely new paradigm of health services. The paradigm included changes in the conceptualisation, planning and delivery, including new ways of health financing. At the same time, epidemiological priorities remained unchanged.

This new paradigm not only created confusion but also raised fears among the common man that the days of State-supported healthcare are over. The Western Model for structural adjustment and health reforms, primarily promoted by the private sector, calls for cuts in public spending on health services, including tertiary level medical care. World Bank officials issue statements asking the Government to strengthen population control and shift curative care to the private sector. Newspapers are writing *sponsored* articles about introduction of cost-recovery mechanisms in public hospitals, defining essential clinical and public health packages etc. in the disguise of expert opinions. This kind of talk has already made considerable damage to the State run healthcare system in the country. The emergence of medical insurance is already loaded with unfavourable consequences, as it would shift the responsibility of medical and public healthcare to households or the household microenvironment. This would be disastrous as it leads to the State eventually abdicating its responsibility for the provision of healthcare, and a majority of households at the subsistence level in India would be left without any life support system.

NIMS held, right since its inception, responsibility to initiate effort to empower the State run healthcare infrastructure with technology and rejuvenate it to effectively support the common man during distress. For various reasons, most health indices remain at unsatisfactory levels. Though so many hospitals mushroomed, the state of preventive medicine and diagnostics is still awry. I knew well that NIMS was expected to not merely function but also to respond to multiple managed care pressures. There were conflicting pressures from the demands of specialised care and its affordability. We had to consolidate as well as upgrade our in-patient operations.

When I was working in Baltimore, there were two area healthcare systems—the two hospital Johns Hopkins Health System, and the 500-physician member Kaiser Permanente Group. We also had three other hospital systems, namely, five-hospital Helix Health System, the academic medical facility, University of Maryland Medicine, and the two-hospital Bon Secours Baltimore Health System. They all worked in tandem as far as the delivery of care to the patient was concerned. There were protocols, parity of tariffs and certain minimal framework of standards that every hospital would adhere to. Here in Hyderabad we had a dozen profit savvy private hospitals all out to capitalise on their investments from patients, two government monoliths settled in their inertia with out-of-order equipment, demoralised physicians and corrupt staffers turned into virtual leeches, and private practitioners running their own queer road shows.

The demands for hospital care can be divided into two categories: community induced demands and the demands influenced by the hospital. The hospital has little or no influence on the amount and range of services provided towards the community induced demand such as first referrals to outpatient clinics, referrals for elective procedures, and referrals for X-rays, laboratory investigations, etc. as requested by community health clinic physicians. In the category of demands influenced by the hospital come range and quantity of services and number of follow-up visits in outpatient clinics, range of services provided in emergency departments and length of hospitalisation stay for non-elective procedures.

Though NIMS was modelled as a referral hospital, hardly any

patient would come with clinical records and a proper work-up. I had to stress upon cutting costs, shortening in-patient stays and transferring patients to less expensive out-patient facilities but also consider the extra burden of someone else's unfinished work on my physicians. There was a virtual stampede because of an increase in direct general patients volume at the expense of serious patients. These patients, always accompanied by at least six attendants, would have no resources to go to private hospitals but would not like to be treated at Government hospitals either. NIMS was increasingly made the target by city-based critics who would complain against lack of attention to someone dear and important to them ignoring the problems peculiar to NIMS.

The influx of technology and hospital-based care brought in complications along. The first casualty was the traditional patient-doctor relationship. It didn't remain a one-on-one affair. The doctor was replaced by a group of physicians, paramedics and administrators. The patient was replaced by referring doctor, attendant, employer and unsolicited lawyer friends. People started talking about hospital mistakes, diagnostic goof-ups and treatment errors. The Andhra Pradesh High Court fired the first salvo against medical practitioners in 1992. A Division Bench in Dr. A.S. Chandra vs. Union of India case held that service rendered for consideration (payment of fees) by private medical practitioners, private hospitals and nursing homes must be construed as "service". However, in 1994 the Madras High Court gave a reprieve of sorts in Dr. C.S. Subramanian vs. Kumarasamy & Anr. Case when it held that services rendered to a patient by a medical practitioner or a hospital by way of diagnosis and treatment both medicinal and surgical would not come within the definition of service. The Court, however, kept paramedical services of all kinds and categories outside this immunity.

In the historic judgment given in Indian Medical Association vs. V.P. Shantha & Ors. in 1995, the Supreme Court of the land held *inter alia* that medical practitioners do not enjoy any immunity and that they can be sued in contract or tort on the ground that they have failed to exercise reasonable skill and care. Only where services are rendered free of charge to every patient, rich and poor alike, or when a medical officer renders such service to his employer under the contract of employment, doctors are given immunity.

What is medical negligence? Negligent action is seen as conduct which falls below the standard established by law for the protection of others against an unreasonable risk of harm. This would imply that the medical professional would become liable for action if the duty of care was owed by the medical professional to the patient and the medical professional violated the applicable standard of care because of which the patient suffered an injury.

The mother of all judgements came in 1996 from the Supreme Court in Poonam Verma vs. Dr. Ashwin Patel case. Here a homeopathic medical practitioner had prescribed allopathic drugs to a patient who succumbed to a "probable infection leading to septicaemia on a background of hitherto unrecognised diabetes mellitus" (a conclusion reached by six experts to whom a reference was made by the Supreme Court). Death in this instance was not due to the drugs prescribed by the homeopathic medical practitioner and also not due to want of care on his part. It was because he prescribed them when he was not supposed to under a statutory law (The Indian Medical Council Act, 1956 prohibits non-MBBS doctors from practising allopathic system of medicine). However, the Honourable Court in its infinite wisdom put it rather simplistically saying: a person who does not have knowledge of a particular system of medicine but practises in that system is a quack and a mere pretender to medical knowledge or skill, or to put it differently, a charlatan. The Court said, "The liability of a doctor in respect of his diagnosis includes his liability to warn patients of the risk inherent in the treatment and his liability in respect of the treatment." The court also chose to clarify that the correct meaning of the impressive Latin maxim—*Sic Utere tuo ut alienum non loedas*—is "Use your property in such manner as not to injure that of another!" The law, however, permits such practitioners of Indian Medicine to make use of modern advances in various sciences such as Radiology, ECG, Blood picture report etc. for the purpose of practising their own system.

In 1998 the Supreme Court in Spring Meadows Hospital v. Harjol Ahluwalia case held that the hospital was also liable for mistakes of its doctors and staff on the principle of *vicarious* liability (when the master is held liable due to a negligent act or omission of his servant). In this case, a child, Harjol Ahluwalia, was left brain damaged after a wrong injection for treatment of typhoid (instead of chloromycetin, chloroquin was injected) was given to him by a nurse who had in turn been instructed to give the injection by the resident doctor. The Court awarded compensation not only to the child who suffered a grave injury but also to his parents who were considered consumers along with the child. The Court, widening the meaning of the victim of a medical error, reasoned that the parents would support the child during its life and also for the mental agony caused to them for the injury of their child.

I wish every physician always remembered the sacred words used by the court: "The relationship between the doctor and the patient is not always equally balanced. The attitude of a patient is poised between trust in the learning of another and the general distress of one who is in a state of uncertainty. Such ambivalence naturally leads to a sense of inferiority and it is, therefore, the function of medical ethics to ensure that the superiority of the doctor is not abused in any manner."

I held detailed discussions with legal experts to go to the bottom of the matter. I am tempted to share some wisdom on this aspect for the day is not far when we will have "medical lawyers" and "hospital courts".

The traditional basis of liability is that there must either be wrongful intent or negligence and this applies to both professionals and non-professionals. From this basic postulate of liability, negligence in the professional and non-professional takes different paths. Men must be able to assume that others will act reasonably and prudently, so as not, by want of due care under the circumstances, to impose upon them an unreasonable risk of injury. In a professional, from this basic principle, the ground of liability is, therefore, failure to come up to the legal standard of due care under the circumstances while carrying on some course of conduct, and so subjecting another to an unreasonable risk, whereby injury is caused.

Negligence under the civil law, whether causing harm short of death or death is fairly well defined and compensatory damages awarded to restore, as far as possible, the sufferer or his relatives by monetary award, as compensation for the harm caused. However, under the criminal law, negligence resulting in death may jeopardise the future of a professional beyond the punishment he has to suffer, if prosecution against him is successful. Denial of a passport to travel, visa refusal to enter a country or removal from professional roster are just a few of the disqualifications a professional is likely to face because of a charge under the Indian Penal Code.

The Penal Code (Section 304-A), however, comes into play only when death is caused. It includes running the risk of the act with recklessness or indifference as to its consequences. Example: a medical practitioner undertakes termination of pregnancy in its sixth month. Here is a rash act where the medical practitioner is aware, or should be (knowledge) that the act is dangerous and could result in death but yet undertakes the termination with indifference to its likely consequences.

Medical professionals are often indifferent to remote and unimportant dangers to which they expose their patients. For example, testing a patient for sensitivity to lignocaine prior to giving a spinal or epidural anesthetic is rarely if ever done. While it is true that allergy to lignocaine is remote, the professional who uses it without testing would be liable for negligence under the civil law. But would this liability extend under the criminal law if death occurs?

It is perfectly reasonable to cast the risk of essentially dangerous conduct (and medical practice is one such conduct) on doctors who pursue it. This may also be an answer to a pressing social need, since a professional may be better able to bear the loss as he can protect himself by a small insurance premium like a person who drives a motor vehicle for pleasure or profit.

I also learned two beautiful Roman phrases from my lawyer friends which I suggest all medical professionals must learn—*Mperitia culpae ad numerator*—lack of experience is a kind of negligence; and—*Magna culpa dolus est*—great negligence is equal to intention. I once visited a medical attorney in New York who displayed in his office these lines which I wish I never see in my own country:

We help you make prepare,
To meet your doctors alike;
When you are anvil bear -
When you are hammer strike.

One day a Swamiji in his saffron attire barged into my cabin. He was very upset about the neglect shown to his suffering disciple. He almost cursed me for compounding the pain of already suffering patients. I refused to get provoked and asked the holy man to take a seat while I gathered facts about the omissions of my people. The patient—a young lady—was suffering from lower back pain. She was also a hypertensive and diabetic. These ailments did not go with her sanctified background. Sometimes minor illnesses prove to be the forewarning of a bigger disaster. "Why don't you help her spiritually?" I asked Swamiji. "Why not you evoke the healer within her?" My honest advice further angered him and he left asking that what was our use if we could not 'fix' simple things.

Can illness be our friend? It can be when it is a way of contacting the physician within. It is some sort of a social communication—a way that the body has of saying both to us and to the world around us—about something that is wrong there. Will you please do something about it? How many of us ignore the symptoms of illness until we are really sick? Most of us! Why? We are often afraid those symptoms may represent something we don't want to know about, and if we don't pay attention to them, they will go away. Like a true ostrich we bury our head in sand wishing the predator will go away. Because of our mindset cast in schools to be like everyone else and feel defensive about being different. We tend to think illness as something of a wrong committed by us and something we must endure in silence. But illness is the body saying "pay attention, help me." If you have a pain in the shoulder, before you gulp a painkiller ask, "Am I shouldering too much?" If you have a pain in the neck, the question can be twofold: "What is it I am being a pain in the neck about?" Or, "Who am I allowing to give me a pain in the neck?" I have thought about pain enough, planning so many surgeries, examining so many cancers, holding so many hands when nothing more could be done.

Nothing can be more untrue than the notion that having a healthy abundant life means a life free of pain. Can it ever happen? Is the pain really an adversary? In reality, it is not the pain that scares us but fear. Gripped by fear we do everything we can to control or moderate our pain and become addicted in that process. What are the most common medications sold in any medical stores beside junk vitamins and tonics? Painkillers and tranquillisers. We want to keep the pain out there, away from us. We think that as long as we don't deal with it, it will go away. What we have to do instead is work with the pain, flow with it and know that at times it is necessary. You may ask which came first? Was it fear or pain? It really doesn't matter. They are together and live in the same house.

In November 1998, Chief Minister Chandra Babu Naidu laid the foundation stone for a Millennium Block in the presence of Health Minister Dr. N. Janardana Reddy. The block was designed to house 86 patients in rooms having comforts and amenities generally available only in high priced corporate hospitals. He provided almost the entire cost of Rs. 5 crores for the project.

Though paramedics play a very crucial role in the delivery of healthcare, they are often taken for granted and are expected to know their skills all the time. Prof. Subbalakshmi Murthy took great pains in organising the first ever State conference of radiographers, dark room assistants and imaging technologists. About 375 delegates attended this educational event. We invited Sri Tridandi Srimannarayana Ramanuja Chinna Jeeyar Swamiji to preside over the function.

I was conferred the Indian Radiologist of the Millennium Award by the Indian Radiological & Imaging Association on January 6, 2000 at Bhopal. On the Republic day I was conferred *Padma Shri* by the nation.

In another development the long-stalled project of setting up a cancer hospital in memory of NTR's wife Basava Tarakamma gained momentum. Dr. Kodela Siva Prasad Rao was personally chosen by NTR to build the hospital in 1984 itself. A trust was created for this purpose with me as a trustee. NTR kept all his sons and daughters out of the trust to ensure that the hospital does not turn into a family enterprise anytime in future. For more than a decade nothing significant happened. After the death of NTR, a distant relative of NTR in the construction industry, P. Venkateswarlu, came forward to construct the hospital building by mobilising necessary resources. He was supported by several donors from Andhra and the United States. Dr. Nori Dattatreyudu was the radiation oncologist for Mrs. Basavatarakamma, who wished a cancer hospital built in Hyderabad for the poor. With Dr. Nori as founder President of American Telugu Women's Association, he roped in several people and initiated to support Basavatarakamma Memorial Cancer Centre. Dr. Tulasi Devi, President of American Telugu Women's Organization and her husband Dr. Polavarapu Raghava Rao worked with missionary zeal to make the hospital happen. They mobilised funds from the American Telugu community to buy Andhra Pradesh's first linear accelerator. This machine can direct electrons and proton beams at cancerous tumours through a pencil thin ray non-invasively without damaging the surrounding healthy tissue. An automated tele-cobalt therapy unit was also installed. Prime Minister Atal Behari Vajpayee inaugurated the hospital on June 22, 2000 in the presence of Chief Minister Chandra Babu Naidu and Bharatiya Janata Party leader M. Venkayya Naidu. "I know intimately the sufferings of cancer. My both parents died with it", Prime Minister said. He also appealed to farmers against growing tobacco, as its consumption is a leading cause of cancer in rural areas. "Ignorance about cancer in our villages must go," said the Prime Minister.

To improve medical care, allopathic doctors working together with colleagues in alternative medicine can eliminate ignorance by sharing information and educating the public at large. This can create real awareness about good health. Respect is the key. We first must respect the diverse ethnic backgrounds of our citizens.

Two men looked through prison bars—
One saw mud, the other stars.

Each patient brings with him a tale to city hospitals from

districts. The tales must be heard. Increasing sophistication in healthcare has certainly failed in creating a safe system of preventive medicine. The solution lies in traditional systems and the tales woven around them. By coming to terms with scientific values and plumbing the depths of natural medicine, we can begin to develop a new humanistic approach to medicine. We can once again begin to give central value to important ethical values such as compassion.

Being the director of NIMS has not been an easy task. Funds from the Govt. are meagre. The staff who worked with enthusiasm and jubilance during my first stint have been permanent fixtures. Instead of working to enhance the image of the Institute, each one had transformed to work for self. Egos have been inflated, jealousies among the faculty have crept in. While the most efficient have gone for greener pastures, the mediocre have been working diligently to improve their mettle and material amenities. A small section has been inciting the class IV and residents to get pay scale of the level of All India Institute of Medical Sciences, New Delhi, which is financially supported by the Central Government. Thus, the salary structure at all levels has been enhanced with a drain on the budget. And yet, the financial support from State Govt. has been meagre. There is a fall upon the cutting down the free and concessional treatment of the poor. Often I reflect myself whether this has been my original objective of returning back and putting a good number of hours in work neglecting my personal health. This 'satisfaction' is the ultimate success for a person with conscience. I have tried to elevate the standards of quality of tertiary care, encouraged post graduate medical education and research and helped many poor patients, coming from far off villages. What more do I want in this short life?

□

PART III

Contemplation

Ellavaariki noka illu manchidi kaldu
Illu joodaga neda talladillu
Talladillinapude tanuvunu marachunu
Tanuvu marachaneni tane Vema.

All men have one excellent dwelling. Beholding this house the heart is afraid when it is in dread. It swoons when the body swoons. Those who forget the body are resolved into great spirit.

Vemana
Verses of Vemana; 523

7

The story of my life reaches the present moment but the story of life continues. Where do we go from here? While we, running hospitals and clinics in India, are busy drowning ourselves in the trivialities of administration and commerce, so much is happening in the world that has the potential of metamorphosing healthcare. The inadequacies of Western Medicine to handle cancer and immunological diseases are obvious. The drug scenario is chaotic to the extent of being scary as one after another version of antibiotic resistant bacteria is knocking off the carefully erected edifices of pharmaceutical industry. The release of human genome map has shaken the basic foundation of medical science: Also has emerged a new interest in heritage systems of healing and a new line of thought that can be termed as evolutionary medicine. In the four chapters of this part I would attempt to put this knowledge together in the form of an outline of the emerging medical science and the contemporary outlook on healthcare.

I am too old to have written this book on paper, get it typed, fish out notes from scientific journals and my own records, put all the text together using scissors and glue. But I had to do nothing of that kind. We keyed in the narration leaning over a lap-top computer, scanned records and downloaded files from the Internet and MedLine, moved paragraphs around swiftly and smoothly using little software icons suitably designed by the creative folks at Microsoft. But the output is the same—a text compiled to carry forward a train of thought. We have created, retrieved, edited and moved so many paragraphs between pages, cut out and pasted them back somewhere else, all of which appears as plain drudgery. Can we edit the text of genes to make a beautiful book of life free from disease and pain?

As the third millennium arrives, we are for the first time in a position to edit the text of our genetic code. It is no longer a sacred manuscript; it is on the floppy as a digital file. We can cut bits out, add bits on, rearrange paragraphs or write over words. Whereas English books are written in words of variable length using 26 letters, genomes are written entirely in three-letter words, using only four letters: *A,C,G* and *T* (which stand for *adenine, cytosine, guanine* and *thymine)*. And instead of on flat pages they are written on long chains of sugar and phosphate called DNA molecules to which bases are attached as side rungs. Each chromosome is a pair of very long DNA molecules.

The genome is a very clever book. In the right conditions it can both photocopy itself and read itself. The photocopying is known as *replication,* and the reading as *translation.* There is little grammar involved. *A* pairs with *T*, and *G* with, *C*. So a single strand of DNA can copy itself by assembling a complementary strand with all *T's* opposite to all *A's*, all *A's* opposite to all *T's*, all *C's* opposite to all *G's* and all *G's* opposite to all *Cs*. This is how the famous *Double Helix* is made of an original strand and its complementary pair intertwined. RNA too carries a linear code using the same letters as DNA except it uses, *U*, for *uracil,* in place of *T*, *thymine.*

To this day, the genetic code consists of three-letter words, each spelling out a particular amino acid as part of a recipe for a protein. As 64 three letter words can be written by four letters and if words containing same three letters (like *AAA, CCC*) and same rotating order are excluded, twenty letters are left. These twenty-three amino acids are the material out of which the whole living world is made of. These three letter words of the amino acids are the same for every creature. *CGA* means *arginine* and *GCG* means *alanine*—in bats, in beetles, in beech trees, in bacteria. Wherever you go in the world, whatever animal, plant, bug, or blob you look at, if it is alive, it will use the same dictionary and know the same code. All life is one. If *seaweed* is man's distant cousin, *anthrax* is his advanced relative. What a great genius poet Erasmus Darwin was, who wrote 200 years back, "One and the same kind of living filaments has been the cause of all organic life."

Life consists of the interplay of two kinds of chemicals: proteins and DNA. Protein represents chemistry, living, breathing, metabolism and behaviour—what biologists call the phenotype. DNA represents information, replication, breeding, sex—what biologists call the genotype. Neither can exist without the other. It is the classic case of chicken and egg: which came first, DNA or protein? It cannot have been DNA, because DNA is a helpless, passive piece of mathematics, which catalyses no chemical reactions. It cannot have been proteins, because protein is pure chemistry with no known way of copying itself accurately. It seems impossible either that DNA invented protein or *vice versa*.

However, we now know that eggs came long before chickens, the reptilian ancestors of all birds laid eggs, so there is growing evidence that RNA came before both DNA and proteins. RNA is a chemical substance that links the two worlds of DNA and protein. It is used mainly in the translation of the message from the alphabet of DNA to the alphabet of proteins. RNA was Greece to DNA's Rome.

We also know that the main purpose of genes is to store the recipe for making proteins. It is proteins that do almost every chemical, structural and regulatory thing in the body. They generate energy, fight infection, digest food, form hairs, carry oxygen and so on and on. Every single protein in the body is made from a gene by a translation of the genetic code.

The complete set of human genes, called genome, comes packaged in twenty-three separate pairs of chromosomes. Of these twenty-two pairs are numbered in approximate order of size, from the largest (number 1) to the smallest (number 22), while the remaining pair consists of the sex chromosomes—two large X chromosomes in women, one X and one small Y in men. In size, the X comes between chromosomes 7 and 8, whereas the Y is the smallest. One set of the genome comes from the mother and one from the father. Each set includes some 30,000 genes arranged into twenty-three chromosomes.

Open any book on human genome and you will be confronted

not with a list of human potentialities, but a list of diseases, mostly once named after pairs of obscure central-European doctors. This gene causes Niemann-Pick disease; that one causes Wolf-Hirschhorn syndrome. The impression given is that genes are there to cause diseases. 'New gene for mental illness', announces a website on genes that reports the latest news from the front, 'The gene for earlyonset dystonia. Gene for kidney cancer isolated. Autism linked to sertonin transporter gene. A new Alzheimer's gene. The genetics of obsessive behaviour.' What on earth is going on?

To define genes by the diseases they cause is about as absurd as defining organs of the body by the diseases they get. Livers are there to cause cirrhosis, hearts to cause angina and brains to cause strokes. It is literally true that the only thing we know about some genes is that their malfunction causes a particular disease. This is pitifully a small thing to know about a gene, and a terribly misleading one. It leads to the dangerous shorthand like "X has got the Wolf-Hirschhorn gene." The fact is that all of us have the Wolf-Hirschhorn gene. The sufferers of Wolf-Hirschhorn Syndrome (facial abnormalities) do not have Wolf-Hirschhorn gene. Those who have a mutated version of this gene suffer from dreaded Huntington's chorea (madness).

Sitting on chromosome 4, the Wolf-Hirschhorn gene contains a single word CAG repeated over and over again—*CAGCAGCAG...* The repetition continues sometimes just six times, sometimes thirty, sometimes more than a hundred times. Our destiny, our sanity and our life hang by the thread of this repetition. If the word is repeated thirty-five times or fewer, one will be fine. Most of us have about ten to fifteen repeats. Anyone having fifty repetitions is destined to lose his mind at roughly 27 years of age. There is nothing one can do about it. It does not matter if you smoke, or take vitamin pills, if you work out or become a couch potato. Is this fate? Science has attained the position of Tiresias, the blind seer of Thebes. By accident Tiresias saw Athena bathing and she struck him blind. Afterwards she repented and, unable to restore his sight, gave him the power of soothsaying. But seeing the future was a terrible fate, since Tiresias could see it but not change it. "It is but sorrow", said Tiresias to Oedipus, "to be wise when wisdom profits not." However, not all that is known and unchangeable is frightening and scary.

On chromosome 9 lies a very well-known gene that determines one's ABO blood group. Roughly 40% Indians have type O blood, 40% have type A blood, 15% have type B blood and 5% have type AB blood. But the native American population was almost exclusively type O, save for some Canadian tribes, who were very often type A, and Eskimos, who were sometimes type AB or B. The *text* of the gene is 1,062 *letters* long, divided into six short and one long *paragraphs* (called *exons*) scattered over the 18,000-letters-long chromosome 9. The difference between the A gene and the B gene is seven letters out of 1,062. Out of the seven, three are synonymous or silent, that is, they make no difference to the amino acid chosen in the protein chain. The four letters that matter are letters at 523, 700, 793 and 800 positions. In people with type A blood these letters read *C,G,C,* and *G*. In people with type B blood they read *G,A,A,* and *C*. Just these four little differences are sufficient to evoke an immune reaction to the wrong blood and kill the recipient!

The O group has just a single spelling change compared with A, but instead of a subsitution of one letter for another, it is a deletion. In people with type O blood, the 258th letter which should read *G*, is missing altogether. Since the genetic code is read in three-letter words and has no punctuation, the absence of just one letter fairly early in the message, makes the whole subsequent message saying something completely different. The AB genotypes offer protection against cholera, the most virulent and lethal of human diseases. People with type O blood seem to be slightly more resistant to malaria than people of other blood groups. They also seem to be slightly less likely to get cancers of various kinds.

Until recently, doctors were in the habit of underestimating the importance of infectious diseases. Many diseases that are generally thought to be due to environmental conditions, occupation, diet or pure chance are now beginning to be recognised as the side-effects of chronic little infections with little known viruses or bacteria. Several drug companies grew rich on new drugs intended to fight the symptoms of ulcers, when all that were needed all along were antibiotics. Ulcers are caused by *Helicobacter Pyroli,* a bacterium usually acquired in childhood and stays there, rather than by rich food, anxiety or misfortune as we were made to believe. Likewise, there are strong suggestive links between heart disease and infection with chlamydia or herpes virus, between various forms of arthritis and various viruses, even between depression or schizophrenia and a rare brain virus called Borna disease virus that usually infects horses and cats. As if, poet John Dryden wrote for the saga of infectious diseases:

Errors, like straws, upon the surface flow;
He who would search for pearls must dive below.

In a sense, the genome is a written record of our pathological past, a medical signature for each people and race. In the scripture that is genome, are written the past history of plagues. The long struggles of our ancestors with malaria and dysentery are recorded in the patterns of human genetic variation. My chances of avoiding death from malaria are pre-programmed in my genes, and in the genes of the malaria organism. When a female anopheles interjects the malaria parasite in my bloodstream my genes play the match with the genes of malaria parasite. If their attackers are better than my defenders, they win and I go. Bad luck. No substitutes allowed.

Take another dreaded substance—Cholesterol—a word pregnant with danger—the cause of heart disease. "You eat it and you die!" Nothing could be more wrong than this equation of cholesterol with poison. Cholesterol is an essential ingredient of the body. It lies in the centre of an intricate system of biochemistry and genetics that integrates the whole body. Cholesterol is a small organic compound that is soluble in fat but not in water. The body manufactures most of its cholesterol from sugars in the diet, and could not survive without it. From cholesterol at least five crucial hormones are made, each with a very different task: progesterone, aldosterone, cortisol, testosterone and oestradiol. Collectively they are known as steroids. The relationship between these hormones and the genes of the body is intimate, fascinating and unsettling.

Steroids have been used by living creatures for so long that they probably pre-date the split between plants, animals and fungi.

The hormone that triggers the shedding of an insect's skin is a steroid. So is the enigmatic chemical known in human medicine as vitamin D. Some synthetic, or anabolic, steroids can be manufactured to trick the body into suppressing inflammations, while others can be used for building athletes' muscles. Yet other steroids, derived originally from plants, can mimic human hormones sufficiently well to be used as oral contraceptives. Beware of certain *Ayurvedic* drugs. All that come from plants is not always safe and without side effects. As much all that glitters is not gold, all that is gold is also not good.

Come to another thoroughly confused area of mental stress. It is supposedly caused by the outside world. An impending exam, a recent bereavement, frightening news or the unremitting exhaustion of living through a bad marriage or caring for old parents sure to die but not passing. Short term stressors cause an immediate increase in epinephrine and norepinephrine, the hormones that make the heart beat faster and feet go cold. Stressors that last longer activate a different pathway that results in a much slower, but more persistent increase in cortisol. One of cortisol's most surprising effects is that it suppresses the working of the immune system. Cortisol reduces the activity, number and lifetime of lymphocytes—the white blood cells guarding against infectious microbes. Cortisol does this by switching certain genes on. One of them is *TCF* on chromosome 10. It is a remarkable fact that students during examination season catch colds and other infections while others in the families remain unaffected.

We are not a brain running a body by switching on hormones. Nor are we a body running a genome by switching on hormone receptors. Nor are we a genome running a brain by switching on genes that switch on hormones. We are all of these at once. The brain, the body and the genome are locked, all three, in a dance. The genome is as much under the control of the other two as they are controlled by it.

Recently, a massive long-term study of 17,000 British civil servants arrived at a startling conclusion about the susceptibility of a person to coronary artery disease. The study reported that somebody in a low-grade job, such as a janitor, was nearly four times as likely to have a heart attack as a permanent secretary at the top of the heap. Indeed, even if the permanent secretary was fat, hypertensive or a smoker, he was still less likely to suffer a heart attack at a given age than a thin, non-smoking, low-blood-pressure janitor. Exactly the same result emerged from a similar study of a million employees of The Bell Telephone Company.

Cholesterol is certainly relegated to the margins of the story. High cholesterol can be a risk factor only in those who have a genetic predisposition to coronary artery disease and in these people the beneficial effects of even eating less fat are small. It also relegated diet, smoking and blood pressure—all the physiological causes cited by the medical profession—to secondary causes. It relegated to a footnote the old and largely discredited notion that stress and heart attacks come with busy, senior jobs or fast-living personalities—though there is a grain of truth in this fact but only a grain! Instead of dwarfing these effects, science now elevates something non-physiological, something so intangible as the status of your job. The cortisol rises in response not to the amount of work one does, but to the degree to which one is ordered about by other people. The extremely controlled people suffer a greater increase in stress hormones and rise in blood pressure and heart rate. The fear of losing a job in the private sector sends more executives to ICCUs than Government officials who at worst might be transferred to a different department.

The new revealed fact that heart disease is a symptom of lack of control explains a good deal about its sporadic appearance. It explains why so many people at senior jobs have heart attacks soon after they retire and 'take it easy'. From running offices they often move to lowly and menial jobs (buying groceries, walking the dog) in domestic environments controlled by their spouses. It explains why people are capable of postponing an illness, even a heart attack, until after a family wedding or a major celebration—until the end of a period of busy work when they are in control of events. It explains why unemployment and decision-dependency are so good at making people ill.

Another hormone that is linked to social status is serotonin. The levels of serotonin are not innate and inflexible. The higher a person has his self-esteem and social rank related to those around him, the higher his serotonin level is. Contrary to what most people think, high rank means low aggressiveness. The high-ranking individuals are not especially large, fierce or violent. They are good at things like reconciliation and recruiting allies. They are notable for their calm demeanour. They are less impulsive, less likely to misinterpret play-fighting as aggression. In university fraternities, the leading figures are blessed with rich sertonin concentrations which fall if they are deposed. Belief in one's low or high serotonin levels could become a self-fulfilling prophecy. The psychological precedes the physical. The mind drives the body, which drives the genome. William Shakespeare writes in King Lear: 'This is the excellent foppery of the world, that, when we are sick in fortune—often the surfeit of our own behaviour—we make guilty of our disasters the sun, the moon, and the stars; as if we were villains by necessity, fools by heavenly compulsion."

If the genome is immortal, why does the body die? Four billion years of continuous photocopying has not dulled the message in our genes, yet the human skin gradually loses its elasticity as we age. It takes fewer than 50 cell doublings to make a body from a fertilised egg and only a few hundred more to keep the skin in good repair. There is an old story that someone in Pedamuttevi told me once. Once King Krishna Devaraya offered to gift Tenali Rama whatever he wanted. The wise Brahmin asked for a chessboard with one grain of rice on the first square, two on the second, four on the third, eight on the fourth and so on. By the tenth square, all the rice in the kingdom goes to Tenali Rama. Thus it is with the human body. The egg divides once, then each daughter cell divides again, and so on. In just 47 doublings, the resulting body has more than 60 trillion cells.

Because some cells cease doubling early and others continue, many tissues are created by more than 50 doublings, and because some tissues continue repairing themselves throughout life, certain cell lines may have doubled several hundred times during a long life. That means their chromosomes have been photocopied several hundred times, enough to blur the message they contain. Yet 50 billion copyings since the dawn of life did not blur the genes we inherited. The difference lies in the shape of a gene TEP_1 that lies on chromosome 14. The product of TEP_1 is a protein, which forms part of a most unusual little biochemical machine called telomerase. Lack of telomerase causes, to put it bluntly, senility. Addition of telomerase turns certain cells immortal.

The story starts with a chance observation in 1972 by James Watson, DNA's discoverer with Francis Crick. Watson noticed that the biochemical machines that copy DNA, called polymerases, cannot start at the very tip of a DNA strand. They need to start several words into the text. Therefore the text gets a little shorter every time it is duplicated. Imagine a photocopier that makes perfect copies of the page but every time you take a copy, the first and the last line go away. The way to cope with such a maddening machine would be to start and end each page with a line of repeated nonsense that you do not mind losing. This is exactly what chromosome does. Each chromosome is just a giant, super-coiled, foot long molecule, so it can all be copied except the very tip of each end. And at the end of the chromosome there occurs a repeated stretch of meaningless text: the word *TTAGGG* repeated again and again about two thousand times. This stretch of terminal tedium is known as *telomere.* Its presence enables the DNA copying devices to get started without cutting short any sense-containing *text.* Like an aglet, the little plastic bit at the end of a shoelace, it stops the end of the chromosome from fraying.

But every time the chromosome is copied, a little bit of the telomere is left off. After a few hundred copyings, the chromosome is getting so short at the end that meaningful genes are in danger of being left off. In our bodies the telomeres shorten at the rate of about 31 letters a year—more in some tissues. That is why cells grow old and cease to thrive beyond a certain age. My telomeres by now should be on average about 5/8th as long as they were when I got them from my parents.

The reason that genes do not get left off in egg cells and sperm cells, the direct ancestors of the next generation, is the presence of telomerase, whose job is to repair the frayed ends of chromosomes and re-lengthen the telomeres. Interestingly the *phrase TTAGGG,* which is repeated a few thousand times in each telomere, is exactly the same in the telomeres of all mammals. Indeed, it is the same in all animals, and even in protozoans that cause sleeping sickness, and in fungi such as *Neurospora.* In plants the phrase has an extra *T* in the beginning: *TTTAGGG.* Telomeres seem to behave like the elixir of eternal life for cells. In normal human development, the genes that make telomerase are switched off in all but a few tissues of the developing embryo. From that moment the telomeres count the number of divisions in each cell and at a certain point they reach their limit and call a halt. The lack of telomerase seems to be the principal reason that cells grow old and die, but is it the principal reason bodies grow old and die? There is some good evidence in favour.

Cells in the walls of arteries generally have shorter telomeres than cells in the walls of veins. This reflects the harder lives of arterial walls, which are subject to more stress and strain because arterial blood is under higher pressure. They have to expand and contract with every pulse beat, so they suffer more damage and need more repair. Repair involves cell copying, which uses up the ends of telomeres. The cells start to age, which is why people die from hardened arteries, not from hardened veins.

There is a great variety in telomere length between different people. The telomere length varies from about 7,000 DNA letters (*A, C, G* and *T*) to about 10,000 per chromosome end. The telomere length seems to be strongly inherited, as is longevity. People from long-lived families, in which members regularly reach ninety, may have longer telomeres that take longer to fray, than the rest of us.

Cancer requires active telomerase. A tumour is invigorated with the biochemical elixier of youth and immortality. It is no accident that the immortal cell lines used by scientists in the laboratory are derived from cancer patients. The most famous of them is the HeLa cell line, originated in the cervical tumour of a patient named Henrietta Lacks, a black woman who died in Baltimore in 1951. Her cancer cells were so wildly proliferative when cultured in the laboratory that they often invade other laboratory samples and take over the *Petri* dish. HeLa cells were used for developing polio vaccines and have gone into space. World-wide, they now weigh more than 400 times Henrietta's own body weight. They are spectacularly immortal. This truly *scientific heroine* is celebrated by the city of Atlanta, which recognised 11 October as Henrietta Lacks Day.

The prime risk of cancer is age. Environmental risk factors, such as cigarette smoking, work in part because they accelerate the ageing process. Smoking damages the lungs, which require repair and repair uses up telomere length, thus making the cells older in telomere terms than they would otherwise be. Tissues that are specially prone for cancer tend to be tissues that do a lot of cell division throughout life either for repair or for other reasons: skin, testis, breast, colon, stomach, and white blood cells.

The longer we live, the more mistakes we accumulate in our genes. Mutation in the TP_{53} gene on chromosome 17 is almost the defining feature of a lethal cancer. In over 90% lung cancers TP_{53} gene is broken. In 55% of all human cancers it is broken. People born with one faulty version of out of the two they inherit, have a 90% chance of getting cancers and usually at an early age.

Take, as an example, colorectal cancer. This cancer begins with a mutation that breaks a tumour-suppressor gene called *APC*. If the developing polyp then suffers a second mutation, jamming on an oncogene called *RAS,* it develops into a so-called *adenoma.* If it then suffers a third mutation breaking another, unidentified tumour suppressing gene, the *adenoma* grows into a more serious tumour. And then comes the danger of a fourth mutation, in the TP_{53} gene, which turns the tumour into a full carcinoma. Similar multi-hit models apply to other kinds of cancer, with TP_{53} gene often making the last but fatal entry in the drama. I have included this model here to emphasise why detecting cancer early in the development of the tumour is so important. The larger a tumour becomes, the more likely it is to suffer the next mutation.

Let us take a closer look at the TP_{53} gene. It is 1,179 *letters* long, and encodes the recipe for a simple protein, p53, that is normally rapidly digested by other enzymes so that it has a half life of only 20 minutes. In this state p53 is inactive. But if it sees bits of broken DNA around p53 like some criminal task force gets alerted and takes charge of the whole cell, mainly by switching on other genes. p53 tells the cells to do one of two things—either to halt proliferation, stop replicating its DNA and pause until repaired; or to kill itself. Another sign of trouble that alerts p53 is if the cell starts to run short of oxygen, which is a diagnostic feature of tumour cells. Inside a growing ball of cancer cells, the blood supply can run short, so the cells begin to suffocate. Malignant cancers get over this problem by sending out a signal to the body to grow new arteries into the tumour. These arteries characteristically grow like a crab-claw that first gave cancer its Greek name.

Little wonder that p53 has earned the nickname of *Guardian Angel* of the Genome. TP_{53} seems to encode the greater good, like a suicide pill in the mouth of a terrorist that is crushed only when the terrorist sees no other escape from being arrested. The suicide of cells in this way is known as apoptosis, from the Greek of the fall of autumn leaves. It is the most important of the body's weapons against cancer, the last line of defence. All therapeutic cancer treatment works only because it induces apoptosis by alerting p53 and its colleagues.

Contrary to the general perception that radiation and chemotherapy preferentially kill cancerous cells by damaging their DNA as it is being copied is far from true. These treatments do induce a little DNA damage but not enough to kill the cells. Instead, the DNA damage is just sufficient to alert p53, which tells the cells to commit suicide. Both radiation and chemotherapy are like vaccination, treatments that work by helping the body to help itself.

These insights are of great importance to the treatment of cancer. A major branch of medicine has been acting under a large misapprehension. Instead of looking for agents that kill dividing cells, doctors should have been looking for agents that encourage cell suicide. I am not saying that chemotherapy has been wholly ineffective, but it has been effective sometimes and only by accident. Now that medical research knows what it is doing, the results should be more promising. In the short term it promises a less painful death for many cancer patients. By testing to see if TP_{53} is already broken, doctors should soon be able to tell in advance if chemotherapy will work. If it will not, then the patient and his family can be spared the expenses, suffering and false hope that is now a feature of the last months of life.

The arrival of newer technology confronts us with a moral dilemma. If the technology can save lives, then not to apply it is morally culpable even if there are attendant risks. For ages there was no option but to watch people die of smallpox but after Jenner had perfected vaccination we were derelict in our duty if we did so. Just fifty years back, people had no alternative to watching their parents succumb to tuberculosis. After Waksma found streptomycin we were guilty of neglect if we failed to take a dying tubercular patient to the doctor. And what applies at the individual level applies with even greater force at the level of countries and societies. Rich countries can no longer ignore the epidemics of diarrhoea that claim the lives of countless children in poor countries, because no longer can we argue that nothing can be done medically. Oral rehydration therapy has given a conscience. Because something can be done, something must be done.

Today the knowledge of genome confronts us with a moral dilemma about genetic diagnosis. Let me take two of the commonest diseases that afflict people, one a swift and merciless killer, the coronary artery disease; the other a slow and relentless thief of memory, Alzheimer's disease. I believe we are in the danger of being too squeamish and too cautious in using knowledge about the genes that influence both diseases, and we, therefore, may commit the moral error of denying people access to life-saving research.

There is a family of genes called the apolipoprotein genes, or *APO* genes. They come in four basic varieties, called A,B,C, and—strangely E, though they are various different versions of each on different chromosomes. The one that interests us most is *APOE,* which happens to lie on chromosome 19. To understand *APOE's* job requires a digression into the habits of cholesterol and triglyceride fats. When we eat a plate of chicken *biryani,* we absorb much fat and with it cholesterol. The liver digests this stuff and feeds it into the bloodstream for delivery to other tissues. Being insoluble in water, both triglyceride fats and cholesterol have to be carried through the blood by proteins called lipoproteins. At the beginning of the journey, laden with both cholesterol and fats, the delivery truck is called VLDL, for very-low-density-lipoprotein.

As it drops off its triglycerides, it becomes low-density lipoprotein, or LDL. Finally, after delivering its cholesterol, it becomes high density lipoprotein, HDL and returns to the liver for a new consignment.

The job of *APOE's* protein, called apo-epsilon, is to effect an introduction between VLDL and a receptor on a cell that needs some triglycerides. *APOB's*, or rather apo-beta's job is to do the same for the cholesterol drop-off. It is easy to see, therefore, that *APOE and APOB* are the prime candidates for involvement in heart disease. If they are not working, the cholesterol and fat stay in the bloodstream and can build up on the walls of arteries as atherosclerosis. Knockout mice with no *APOE* genes get atherosclerosis even on a normal mouse diet.The genes for the lipoproteins themselves and for the receptors on cells can also affect the way in which cholesterol and fat behave in the blood and thereby facilitate heart attack. An inherited predisposition to heart disease, called familial hypercholesterolaemia, results from a rare *spelling change* in the gene for cholesterol receptors. What marks *APOE* out as special is that it is so polymorphic. Instead of us all having one version of the gene, it comes in three common kinds, known as E_2, E_3, and E_4. Because these three vary in their efficiency at removing triglycerides from the blood, they also vary in their susceptibility to heart disease. Persons having two copies of E_2 are at markedly higher risk of early heart disease. They are acutely sensitive to fatty and cholesterol-rich diets, or to put it in another way they can be easily treated by being warned against such diets. This is extremely valuable genetic knowledge. How many lives could be saved, and early heart attacks averted, by simple genetic diagnosis to identify those at risk and target treatment at them? Cardiologists have amassed good wealth in India. Why not they sponsor mass *APOE* screening in the hospitals and communities they patronise?

I did not bring in the *APOE* here in the book to write about heart disease. The reason that *APOE* is the most investigated gene of all is not because of its role in the heart disease, but because of its pre-eminent role in a much more sinister and much less curable condition—Alzheimer's disease. The devastating loss of memory and of personality that accompanies old age in so many people has been attributed to all sort of factors, environmental, pathological and accidental. The diagnostic symptom of Alzheimer's disease is the appearance in brain cells of plaques of insoluble protein whose growth damages the cell. A viral infection was once suspected to be the cause, as was a history of frequent blows to the head. The presence of aluminium in the plaques threw suspicion on aluminium cooking pots for a while. In early 1990s at least three genes had been associated with early onset of Alzheimer's disease and quite soon the culprit was discovered to be none other than *APOE* itself. The association of a blood-lipid gene should not have come as such a surprise as it did. After all it is well established clinical knowledge that Alzheimer's victims quite often had high cholesterol. Nonetheless the scale of the effect came as a shock. The bad version of the gene came out to be E_4. If someone carries two E_4 genes his chances of eventually getting Alzheimer's disease are much greater than those of the population at large.

I was wondering why then E_4 exists at all? If it exacerbates both heart disease and Alzheimer's, it should surely have been driven extinct by the more benign E_3 and E_2 long ago. But then I realised that high-fat diets were until very recently so rare, that the coronary side-effects were of little importance. The Alzheimer's disease is all but irrelevant to natural selection, since it not only happens to people who have long ago reared their own children to independence, but strikes at an early age when most Stone Age folks were long dead anyway.

Now let's come to the point. When asked if we should offer *APOE* tests to individuals curious to know if they will get Alzheimer's disease in England, most in the medical profession said no. To test somebody for a disease that is incurable is dubious at best. Since there is no cure, one should not be offered the test unless one is already symptomatic. There is a regrettable tendency among doctors to stick to the *status quo,* to remain within familiarity.

Heaven from all creatures hides the book of fate,
All but the page prescribed, their present state.

To seek out the genes that influence personality, the focus is shifted from the hormones of the body to the chemicals of the mind. On the short arm of chromosome 11, lies a gene called *D_4DR*. It is the recipe for a protein called a dopamine receptor, and it is switched on in cells of certain parts of the brain but not in others. Its job is to stick out of the membrane of a neuron at the junction with another neuron, known as synapse, ready to latch onto a small chemical called dopamine. Dopamine is a neurotransmitter, released from the tips of other neurons by the electrical signal. When the dopamine receptor encounters dopamine, it causes its own neuron to discharge an electric signal of its own. That is the way the brain works—electrical signals that cause chemical signals that cause electrical signals.

The presence of an active *D_4DR* gene in a neuron immediately identifies that neuron as a member of one of the brain's dopamine mediated pathways. Dopamine pathways do many things including the flow of blood through the brain. A shortage of dopamine in the brain causes an indecisive and frozen personality, unable to initiate even body's own movement. In the extreme form, this is known as Parkinson's disease, characterised by unstoppable shaking of hands. Mice with the genes for making dopamine knocked out will starve to death from sheer immobility. An excess of dopamine in the brain, by contrast, makes a mouse highly exploratory and adventurous.

The *D_4DR* gene has a variable repeat sequence in the middle. A *phrase* of forty-eight letters in length is repeated between two and eleven times. Most of us have four or seven copies of the sequence, but some people have two, three, five, six, eight, nine, ten or eleven. The larger the number of repeats, the more ineffective are the dopamine receptors at capturing dopamine. A long *D_4DR* gene implies a low response to dopamine in certain parts of the brain, while a short *D_4DR* gene implies a high responsiveness. Long *D_4DR* gene people need to take a more adventurous approach to life to get the same dopamine *buzz* that short-gened people get from simple things. In search of these buzzes they develop novelty-seeking personalities. They have more sexual partners and maintain an outwardly disposition towards life. Nobody doubts that genes can shape anatomy. The idea that they also shape behaviour needs a lot more swallowing.

So, here we are. At their birth, new technologies often seem hopelessly impractical and too abstract to be competitive to what is being practised. Only gradually and with time does the new invention raise its efficacy to the point where it can match the old. So it is with the emerging knowledge about genome. Protein therapy had won the race to cure severe combined immune deficiency (SCID), which robbed children incapable of mounting an immune defence against infections causing rapid death of all white blood cells. For years poor children died and rich ones kept inside incubators or given a complete bone marrow transplant from a fortunately matched relative. But even the protein therapy required painful monthly injections into the hip, which is expensive and needed to continue for life. We now know that the disease is caused by a spelling change in a single gene on chromosome 20, called the *ADA* gene, It will not be many years from now when it will be possible to edit the spelling mistake. This is not yet possible. These are early days in gene therapy but the day gene therapy could be made to work, it would replace all the pain of monthly injections with a single treatment that would re-equip the body with the gene it should have had in the first place. As for now, genetic diagnosis followed by conventional cure is probably the genome's greatest boon to medicine.

□

8

I am not comfortable with the emergence of excessive and fragmentary form of intervention in contemporary healthcare. It needs to be moderated. The healthcare should shift towards the kind of therapy practised by wise physicians and healers for centuries—a subtle interference with the organism to stimulate it in a specific way so that it will, by itself, complete the process of healing. Therapies should be based on a profound respect for self-healing rather than a contempt towards the organism for certain performance failure. Doctors have taken over a lot of authority which needs to be delegated to the patient in the form of a responsibility to initiate the process of getting well as an act of will.

Before the advent of the AIDS epidemic, not much was heard about the immune system. It was largely considered to be something in the body that was relatively unimportant, as antibiotic drugs were thought to be able to solve most health problems. To the extent that, in 1969, the Surgeon General of the United States, William Stewart, declared that "The war against infectious diseases has been won!"

How wrong he was! The antibiotics developed over the last 30 years since that premature announcement have not destroyed the source of diseases (microbes). What is worse, these lowlifes have mutated, rendering most of even super drugs impotent against the microbes they were designed to kill. Hospitals are now the major source of infection from these mutated microbes because of their heavy use of antibiotics. Even the most powerful drugs are unable to kill these *super bugs*.

But there is now a growing realism amongst open-minded medical researchers that the body's immune system is the most important and only element in the fight against diseases, and that drugs are not the answer. This realisation has not become conventional wisdom because the whole medical industry is built upon the assumption that drugs can cure diseases and too much has been invested in the pharmaceutical industry to support this wrong assumption. Profits from the industry are just too great, as are those in the media, that benefits from their advertisements. To admit that this whole industry is built on such a shaky assumption could lead to the collapse of the industry, in much the same way that the tobacco industry is having to face up to the truth and the economic realities that flow from the truth being known. This is not about to happen to the medical industry anytime soon, as there is too much vested interest in maintaining the myth, including the vested interest in the very lucrative medical research industry that is dedicated exclusively to developing drug therapy.

There are very important reasons for the reluctance of the medical industry to face the truth openly. As natural substances cannot be patented there are no profits to be made out of research into the effectiveness of any natural substance because competitors can then replicate the product. This is not to say pharmaceutical research is not undertaken on the ingredients of plants and other natural substances. It is—in great amounts. If a natural substance is identified as being effective, the laboratory embarks on an analysis to identify if there is a single chemical in this substance which can be replicated (synthesised) in the laboratory. It can then be patent protected, and marketed after research, "due diligence" is undertaken to get Drug Controller's approval. This can cost Rs. 1 to 10 crores! Not many seem to be willing to wait.

There are two technical problems with this approach. The first is that natural substances are bundled together in a way that the body understands, and is able to use. The effectiveness of a single substance is usually far less than a natural bundle, for reasons not fully understood yet. For example, most if not all-synthetic vitamins (vitamin C is an exception) are single substances, lacking the catalysts present in natural vitamins. This largely explains why medical research in the use of vitamins usually comes out negative. The research seldom, if ever, draws a distinction between synthetic and natural vitamins, and synthetics are used in most studies. The industry firmly believes there is no difference.

The second is the mirror image effect. Virtually all-synthetic substances turn out to be mirror images of the natural product they are designed to replicate. Their chemical composition may be identical, but their molecular arrangement is mirrored. This is important, as a natural substance is effective because of its molecular relationship to cells in the body—the lock and key effect. Mirror images do not key with the same locks as natural ones.

All women like their mirror images.
That is their tragedy.
No man does. That is his.

I can tell you from my experience that only the body's iminune system can cure a disease; physicians and alternative medicine practitioners can only assist the body to do this; and natural supplements are superior to drugs in strengthening the immune system. But while I say this I must also share with you the reasons for saying so.

The human body is the wonderful result of millions of years of evolution. We share our DNA with all living creatures, and the fact that we are here today is the result of the incredible capacity of the body to deal with millions of microbes: bacteria, viruses and fungi that cohabit this beautiful world with us. The body is able to survive the onslaught of these potential pathogens because its immune system recognises them, and produces antibodies to immobilise them for removal from the body when they multiply above a level of equilibrium. The immune system can often be disturbed by chemical toxins in the system which place demands on it which it cannot readily meet, as the body has yet to come up with a valid way of identifying and removing modern chemicals.

When a baby is born, its immune system is poorly developed, as it has not been exposed to the pathogens around it. Substances such as Lactoferrin and MSM in the mother's milk are important elements in building the new system and preparing it for a germ-filled world. The system matures and peaks in mid twenties in most people, coinciding with the peaking of their hormones. From then on, it's downhill all the way to old age, when most immune systems are compromised due to bad living habits and exposure to chemicals. It is in one's later years that the condition of the immune system has a great bearing on health, and it is in this period that it is mostly in need of support.

The immune system is composed of many interdependent cell types that collectively protect the body from bacterial, parasitic, fungal, viral infections and from the growth of tumour cells. Many of these cell types have specialised functions. The cells of the immune system can engulf bacteria, kill parasites or tumour cells, or kill viral-infected cells. Often, these cells depend on the T helper subset for activation signals in the form of secretions formally known as cytokines, lymphokines, or more specifically interleukins.

All the cells of the immune system are initially derived from the bone marrow. They form through a process called hematopoiesis *(hemo* is blood, *poiesis* is making). During hematopoiesis, bone marrow derived stem cells differentiate into either mature cells of the immune system or into precursors of cells that migrate out of the bone marrow to continue their maturation elsewhere. The bone marrow produces B cells, natural killer cells, granulocytes and immature thymocytes, in addition to red blood cells and platelets.

Thymus produces mature T cells. Immature thymocytes, also known as prothymocytes, leave the bone marrow and migrate into the thymus. Through a remarkable maturation process sometimes referred to as thymic education, T cells that are beneficial to the immune system are spared, while those T cells that might evoke a detrimental auto-immune response are eliminated. The mature T cells are then released into the bloodstream.

The spleen is an immunologic filter of the blood. It is made up of B cells, T cells, macrophages, dendritic cells, natural killer cells and red blood cells. In addition to capturing foreign materials (antigens) from the blood that passes through the spleen, migratory macrophages and dendritic cells bring antigens to the spleen via the bloodstream. An immune response is initiated when the macrophage or dendritic cells present the antigen to the appropriate B or T cells. This organ can be thought of as an immunological conference centre. In the spleen, B cells become activated and produce large amounts of antibody. Also, old red blood cells are destroyed in the spleen.

The lymph nodes function as an immunologic filter for the bodily fluid known as lymph. Lymph nodes are found throughout the body. Composed mostly of T cells, B cells, dendritic cells and macrophages, the nodes drain fluid from most of our tissues. Antigens are filtered out of the lymph in the lymph node before returning lymph to the circulation. In a similar fashion as the spleen, the macrophages and dendritic cells that capture antigens present these foreign materials to T and B cells, consequently initiating an immune response.

The T lymphocytes are usually divided into two major subsets that are functionally and phenotypically (identifiably) different. The T helper subset, also called the CD4+ T cell, is a pertinent coordinator of immune regulation. The main function of the T helper cell is to augment or potentiate immune responses by the secretion of specialised factors that activate other white blood cells to fight off infection.

Another important type of T cell is called the T killer or suppressor subset or CD8+ T cell. These cells are important in directly killing certain tumour cells, viral-infected cells and sometimes parasites. The CD8+ T cells are also important in down-regulation of immune responses. Both types of T cells can be found throughout the body. They often depend on the secondary lymphoid organs (the lymph nodes and spleen) as sites where activation occurs, but they are also found in other tissues of the body, most conspicuously the liver, lung, blood and intestinal and reproductive tracts.

The Natural Killer cells, often referred to as NK cells, are similar to the killer T cell subset (CD8+ T cells). They function as effector cells that directly kill certain tumours such as melanomas, lymphomas and viral-infected cells, most notably herpes and cytomegalovirus infected cells. NK cells, unlike the CD8+ (killer) T cells, kill their targets without a prior "conference" in the lymphoid organs. However, NK cells that have been activated by secretions from CD4+ T cells kill their tumour or viral-infected targets more effectively.

The major function of B lymphocytes is the production of antibodies in response to foreign proteins of bacteria, viruses and tumour cells. Antibodies are specialised proteins that specifically recognise and bind to one particular protein. Antibody production and binding to a foreign substance or antigen, often is critical as a means of signalling other cells to engulf, kill or remove that substance from the body.

Another group of white blood cells is collectively referred to as granulocytes or polymorphonuclear leukocytes (PMNs). Granulocytes are composed of three cell types identified as neutrophils, eosinophils and basophils, based on their staining characteristics with certain dyes. These cells are predominantly important in the removal of bacteria and parasites from the body. They engulf these foreign bodies and degrade them using their powerful enzymes.

Macrophages are important in the regulation of immune responses. They are often referred to as scavengers or antigen-presenting cells (APC) because they pick up and ingest foreign materials and present these antigens to other cells of the immune system such as T cells and B cells. This is one of the important first steps in the initiation of an immune response. Stimulated macrophages exhibit increased levels of phagocytosis and are also secretory.

Another cell type, addressed only recently, is the dendritic cell. Dendritic cells, which also originate in the bone marrow, function as antigen presenting cells (APC). These cells are usually found in the structural compartment of the lymphoid organs such as the thymus, lymph nodes and spleen. However, they are also found in the bloodstream and other tissues of the body. It is believed that they capture antigen or bring it to the lymphoid organs where an immune response is initiated. Unfortunately, one reason we know so little about dendritic cells is that they are extremely hard to isolate, which is often a prerequisite for the study of the functional qualities of specific cell types. Of particular issue here is the recent finding that dendritic cells bind high amount of HIV, and may be a reservoir of virus that is transmitted to CD4+ T cells during an activation event.

An immune response to foreign antigen requires the presence of an antigen-presenting cell (APC), (usually either a macrophage or dendritic cell) in combination with a B cell or T cell. When an APC presents an antigen on its cell surface to a B cell, the B cell is signalled to proliferate and produce antibodies that specifically bind to that antigen. If the antibodies bind to antigens on bacteria or parasites it acts as a signal for peripheral blood mononuclear cells (pmns) or macrophages to engulf (phagocytose) and kill them. Another important function of antibodies is to initiate the "complement destruction cascade." When antibodies bind to cells or bacteria, serum proteins called complement bind to the immobilised antibodies and destroy the bacteria by creating holes in them. Antibodies can also signal natural killer cells and macrophages to kill viral or bacterial-infected cells.

If the APC presents the antigen to T cells, the T cells become activated. Activated T cells proliferate and become secretory in the case of CD4+ T cells, or, if they are CD8+ T cells, they become activated to kill target cells that specifically express the antigen presented by the APC. The production of antibodies and the activity of CD8+ killer T cells are highly regulated by the CD4+ helper T cell subset. The CD4+ T cells provide growth factors or signals to these cells to proliferate and function more efficiently.

One possible line of therapy is to reintroduce some of these cytokines to people who have severe immune deficiencies. This approach can be tricky because large amounts of any particular cytokine can have serious side-effects. Furthermore, their half-life in the body is usually relatively short. Another shortcoming of "replacement" therapy is that many cytokines will activate the CD4+ T cells or macrophages harbouring HIV, and this could lead to faster rates of HIV production by those cells. Theoretically, this could lead to progression of HIV rather than prophylaxis against opportunistic infections. However, recent progress in this area warrants attention and further study. Lack of interleukin-2 (IL-2) is believed to be one of the major causes of immune deficiency in

AIDS. In recent studies where low dose IL-2 was administered to people with HIV, CD4 T cell counts rose, as did anti-viral specific immunity, and natural killer cell cytotoxic activity. Administration of IL-3 to people with HIV is currently under investigation as a treatment for HIV associated cytopenia (low production of cells from the bone marrow).

IL-4, a cytokine that activates B cells and also has inhibitory effects on the production of Tumour Necrosis Factor (TNF), is currently under investigation for the treatment of Kaposi's sarcoma. Another growth factor GMCSF (granulocyte macrophage-colony stimulating factor) produced by CD4+ T cells, is under investigation for the treatment of decreased white blood cell production for people on ganciclovir therapy. Aditionally, IFN-gamma (gamma interferon) is under investigation as a treatment for people with Pneumocystis Carinii Pneumonia (PCP). Hopefully, these studies will lead to cures for certain opportunistic infections, or for use in inhibiting HIV production and ultimately saving lives.

Armed with this knowledge, the medical science is now seeing diseases in the body as symptoms that occur as the result of a weakened immune system not being able to produce sufficient antibodies to counter a particular strain of virus, bacteria or fungus. The symptoms could be pain, swelling, infected wounds, poor digestion, stiff joints, weakened bones or just general debilitation.

Symptoms are not diseases in themselves—just the body's early warning system to alert us to a problem. If we neglect these warnings or worse, turn them off with drugs like painkillers that suppress the symptoms, the basic problem remains. This is analogous to turning off a screaming smoke detector because the sound is annoying. The result could be that the house burns to the ground unless you seek out the cause of the smoke and extinguish it.

To root out the cause of the symptoms, the immune system must be mobilised to produce sufficient numbers of the correct type of antibodies to destroy the pathogens causing the symptoms before they spread to other areas of the body. The pattern for these antibodies resides in a data base, mapped from previous exposure to the pathogen. A mutated type of flu virus, for instance, might not have been mapped, so this flu has a better chance of taking over a body with a weakened immune system than one the body has successfully dealt with before.

Inoculation is an attempt by the medical industry to provide the body with a complete library of the antibodies of major infective diseases. The problem is to ensure that they don't kill the recipient. Most inoculations are made using animal look-a-likes in dead cell form. They are close enough to the natural pathogen to enable antibodies against them to be developed by the body. They can also be devastating to a body with a poor immune system, diverting resources away from defending the body against present threats to its health to build antibodies against some disease it may never meet. In extreme cases, they can kill the person receiving the inoculation. There is strong evidence from research done in England that Autism in children can result from inoculations. I hope that this is not true, but in time this could be confirmed.

How do you ensure you have a healthy immune system? This may seem contradictory, but the first rule is to stay healthy! If you are constantly tending your health through sensible living habits you need not fuss too much about your immune system as you know it is in good shape. To help you do this, here are some pointers: Keep your digestive system working well. It is one of the most vital parts of the body, capable of eliminating most pathogens from your body when it is healthy! Be careful what chemicals you come into contact with, and stay away from all of them where you have a choice. If the chemical is designed to kill insects or bacteria, it will harm you and damage your body's ability to fight infection. This includes prescription drugs, insecticides, food preservatives, and most cosmetic products. Eliminate all contact with heavy metals from your life, especially amalgam fillings in your teeth. Provide your body with the nutrition it needs to support the immune system. This is the body's only source of material for building health. Support the strength of an older system by using a good quality human growth hormone which has been shown to enhance the IGF-1 factor in the blood. When you feel you need to boost your immune system, use a natural proven product. Do not resort to prescription drugs unless your condition is life threatening. Observe good habits of hygiene, but keep away from anti-bacterial soaps and detergents, which are just a sales gimmick. Your body needs contact with common bacteria in order to recognise new strains, and these new detergents have been shown to help create mutant bacteria.

Our immune systems are set up in such a way that they expect to be educated by soil mycobacteria early in childhood. When they are denied this education the result is an unbalanced immune system prone to allergy. Writes Hamilton in the 18 July 1998 issue of *New Scientist,* "Throw away that water steriliser and seek out mycobacteria."

Fear is the most malignant thing that has plagued mankind since time began. Fear mauls and mutilates us, not killing us outright but letting us live on half a heart and half a lung. How simple it now seems that our ancestors stood outside their caves guarding against the fangs and claws of predators. The evil we must stand vigilant against is like a virus starting from deep inside us, eating its way out. As poet Alfred Tennyson writes:

But what am I?
An infant crying in the night?
An infant crying for the light:
And with no language but a cry!

Surprisingly small shifts in the mind's operations can change us greatly. There is a strong movement emerging about mind-body medicine. Unfortunately this is limited to a few isolated efforts and no institution has come forward to take it up seriously and scientifically. Psychiatry and medicine live like an estranged couple in India. There is mutual contempt between psychiatrists and physicians. I hope something will happen in future. But nevertheless there is a lot of promise in this for cancer patients who hardly had anything new coming from the doctors in the past one decade. I have always respected the powers of mind over body and hence the important role psychologists can play in healing and alleviating pain. So that a few souls can get on to it, I am putting my thoughts.

Psychology as a science is commonly believed to date from

nineteenth century, and its historical roots are usually traced back to Greek antiquity. I find this view rather narrow and culturally conditioned. It's a fact that Sigmund Freud, working in the clinic, used the method of free association to develop psychoanalysis. However Indian system of thought exhibits a variety of profound and sophisticated approaches to psychology. The rich tradition of Indian philosophy has generated a spectrum of philosophical schools, from extreme materialism to extreme idealism, from absolute monism through dualism to complete pluralism. Accordingly, these schools have developed numerous and often conflicting theories about human behaviour, the nature of consciousness and the relation between mind and matter.

In addition to this wide range of philosophical schools, Indian cultures have also developed spiritual traditions that are based on empirical knowledge and thus more akin to the approach of modern science. These traditions are grounded in mystical experiences that have led to elaborate and extremely refined models of consciousness that is in surprising agreement with recent scientific developments. Indian mystical traditions are not, however, primarily concerned with theoretical concepts. They are, above all, ways of liberation, concerned with the transformation of consciousness. Traditions like Vedanta, Yoga, Jainism and Buddhism resemble psychotherapies rather than religions or philosophies.

The speculations of ancient Greek philosophers show strong influences of Indian ideas. One of the most powerful and influential images of the psyche is found in Plato's philosophy. In the Phaedrus, the soul is pictured as a charioteer driving two horses, one representing the bodily passions and the other higher emotions. This metaphor encapsulates the two approaches to consciousness—the biological and the spiritual—which have been pursued, without being reconciled, throughout Western philosophy and science.

I heard a Brother once telling children in our school something like this: "When we die and go to heaven, and we meet our Maker, our Maker is not going to say to us, why didn't you become a messiah? Why didn't you discover the cure for such and such?" The only thing we're going to be asked at that precious moment is, "why didn't you become you?" God treats us as the potter treats his clay. He moulds us into different shapes and sizes. He works some into stout bowls and others into delicate urns. But sometimes he doesn't like what he sees, so he scraps the clay and starts again." What a wonderful message Brother was giving. I wish I could have said to my patients with a little of such eloquence that God is firmly set on making something beautiful and useful out of our lives, no matter how long it takes. And because God never gives up on us, we ought never give up on ourselves. The metaphor of potter is to emphasise the importance of keeping on trying. The only unforgivable sin is giving up on life when a certain disease has made a mess of things.

A number of therapeutic models and techniques are already being developed that go beyond the biomedical framework and are consistent with the systems view of health. The medical establishment does not take most of these models very seriously because they are difficult to understand in terms of classical scientific concepts. Let us dwell upon them a bit.

The emerging unorthodox approaches to health share a belief in the existence of patterns of 'subtle energies' or 'life energies,' and see illness as resulting from changes in these patterns. Although the therapies practised in these traditions, which are sometimes referred to as 'energy medicine,' involve a variety of techniques, all of them are believed to influence the organism at a more fundamental level than the physical or psychological symptoms of illness. It is believed that there are patterns of energy flow and fluctuation in the human organism. It is also believed that 'life energy' is exchanged between an organism and its environment, and many traditions hold that the laying-on of hands and other techniques of *psychic* healing can transfer this energy between human beings. A nine-year-young boy suffering from thalassemia once sent me a letter:

If you touch me soft and gentle
If you look at me and smile
If you listen to me talk sometimes before you talk
I will heal, certainly heal
I will get up, I will walk.

It is such intangible things, love in many forms, which enter into every therapeutic relationship. It is an element of which the physician may be the carrier and the vessel. And it is an element, which binds and heals, which comforts and restores, which surely works. Communications to the inner self take many forms. Our feelings are our primary means of communication with the inner self—feeling aroused by the touch of someone's hand, the sound of music, the smell of a flower, a beautiful sunset, a work of art, love, laughter, hope and faith

Most approaches to *energy medicine* sound vague, simplistic, and often rest on some flimsy scientific basis. However, the founders and practitioners of these healing traditions often had a remarkable intuition for the nature of life, health and illness, and many of their concepts are likely to be extremely useful when reformulated in the language of the new systems approach. I find the term *energy* as used in the emerging unorthodox healing traditions rather problematic from the scientific point of view. Life *energy* is often thought as some kind of substance, which flows through the organism and is transferred between organisms. According to modern science, energy is not a substance but rather a measure of activity, of dynamic patterns. I strongly feel a need to understand the models of 'energy medicine' scientifically, concentrating on the concepts of flow, fluctuation, vibration, rhythm, synchrony and resonance, which in fact form the systems view. Concepts like 'subtle bodies' or 'subtle energies' should not be taken to refer to underlying substances but as metaphors describing the dynamic patterns of self-organisation.

One of the most intriguing approaches to the fundamental dynamic patterns of the human organism is that of Homeopathy. The roots of Homeopathic philosophy can be traced back to Hippocrates, but the German physician Samuel Hahnemann founded the formal therapeutic system at the end of the eighteenth century. Although vigorously opposed by the medical establishment, Homeopathy spread steadily. In the Homeopathic view, illness results from changes in an energy pattern or *vital force,* which is the basis of all physical, emotional and mental phenomena and is characteristic of each individual. The aim of Homeopathic therapy is to stimulate a person's energy levels. In the recent years George Vithoulkas identified Hahnemann's vital force with the body's electromagnetic field and uses the term 'dynamic plane' for the fundamental level at which illness originates. In his theory the dynamic plane is characterised by a pattern of vibration, and these changes generate physical, emotional and mental symptoms.

Homeopathic therapy consists of matching the pattern of symptoms that is characteristic of the patients with a similar pattern characteristic of the remedy. It is believed that each remedy is associated with a certain vibration pattern that constitutes its very essence. When the remedy is taken, its energy pattern resonates with the energy pattern of the patient and thereby induces the healing process. The resonance phenomena seem to be central to Homeopathic therapy, but what exactly resonates and how this resonance is brought about is not well understood. Homeopathic remedies are substances derived from animals, plants and minerals, and are taken in a highly diluted form. It is believed that any substance that can produce a total pattern of symptoms in a healthy human being can cure those same symptoms in a sick person.

The lack of any scientific explanation of Homeopathic therapy is one of the main reasons why it has remained a highly controversial healing art. However, further development of psychosomatic medicine and the systems approach to health will help clarify many of the Homeopathic principles and may well encourage the medical profession to re-examine its position. I personally have great regard for Homeopathic philosophy and its general view of illness, its emphasis on individual treatment and its basic trust in the human organism. I am, however, skeptical about the substances used to create the crucial resonance and wonder whether it is not the one between the patient and the doctor, with the remedy merely a crutch.

The essential foundation of mind-body medicine is the recognition that for every experience in the mind, there is a corresponding change in the physiology and biochemistry of our body. We have a vast internal pharmacy that can be accessed through conscious choices we make in our lives. A key tenet of mind-body medicine is that health is not the mere absence of disease. Rather, it is the dynamic integration of our environment, body, mind and spirit. Reducing stress through meditation techniques, improving vitality through balanced nutrition, and developing flexibility, energy and endurance through yoga and exercise are a few of the basic approaches of mind-body medicine, which have demonstrable health enhancing effects. Herbal medicine, massage, sound, movement and aroma-therapy are other tools of mind-body medicine that can advance mental and physical well-being. Mind-body medicine offers new possibilities for stimulating body's intrinsic healing system.

Almost every doctor would advise his patient not to worry and feel depressed about his problem and pain. How easy it is for him to say but how difficult it is for the patient to follow! There is no way one can avoid emotions, doctors included. Emotions are an essential element of the human condition. When there is a major crisis in our lives, however, our ups and downs are more pronounced. Instead of being able to flow back and forth with the tides of each day, it is more as though we're standing on a rocky shore with waves crashing around us. As if life is an onion, you peel off one layer at a time, and sometimes you weep.

I feel people carry with them anger, depression, frustration, insecurity and anxiety and many other kinds of negative emotions but feel shy of sharing. Some shut themselves up from everyone else because cancer has intruded into their lives. Unfortunately I and most of the doctors treating them would not have time to support their patience and boost their courage. How do they find peace and calm, in their impossible situations? Just because someone has a life-challenging illness, or is concerned about someone who does, how does it automatically grant him a major change in personality or the ability to cope as well as he would like? Like everyone else, when he faces the future he brings his past with him. The strengths he had before, he still has. What bothered him before will bother him now. There is a lot to be said for simple saying, "This is me. I don't intend to change."

Immediately after the initial diagnosis, the patient's attention is focused on making decisions in adjusting to this new reality in his life. However as things settle down a little, he may discover, as thousands of others, that facing a serious illness can be a catalyst for change. How do we help a cancer patient deal with unwanted emotions and expand his life into new ways of being in the world. If nothing else, by working on some of his communication, relationship and emotional issues, he will be able to handle them more effectively under the strain of treatment and the fear of recurrence after remission.

The notion that negative emotions are certainly bad for the immune system, and positive emotions are beneficial is simplistic, inadequate and unsubstantiated. Instead, I feel that emotions in and of themselves are neutral, but, when used in their proper context as necessary information, they help in the process of fighting disease and/or healing. The ancient idea that attitudes play a vital part in the recovery process is finding systematic verification in current medical research.

There is little doubt that fear is a great accelerator of disease. Conversely, hope, faith, confidence and the will to live promote recovery. One of the most fascinating observations of the mind-body correlation was first noticed more than a decade ago. Some multiple personalities that were allergic to strawberries or exhibited symptoms of insulin-dependent diabetes when expressing one personality did not have those physical problems when in another personality state—entirely different reactions within the same body!

Then there is the famous *placebo* response, which is just another way of saying that some people get better simply because they believe they will get better. One of the most frequently cited clinical cases is that of a patient with lymphosarcoma. His condition, thought to be pre-terminal, went into remission almost totally for two months while he received injections of Krebiozen, an experimental drug he thought would cure him. After learning from the news that the drug was useless, he relapsed. His physician cleverly reactivated the patient's faith in the medication by giving him water injections that were described as a refined and more potent form of the same drug. The patient once again recovered, only to relapse and die several months later after discovering from a nation-wide announcement that Krebiozen had no therapeutic value.

disease, the *positive* avoiders, who either rejected the diagnosis or minimised its seriousness, the *stoics,* who accepted the diagnosis but did not seek further information and adopted a fatalistic attitude, and lastly the *helpless and hopeless* whose lives were preoccupied with cancer and dying.

At the end of five years, only 20% of the *helpless and hopeless* group were alive and disease-free. This compared with 32% of the *stoics,* 70% of the *positive avoiders* and a full 80% of the *fighting spirit.* A 10-year follow-up indicated that a fighting spirit was still significantly associated with a better prognosis. This seemed to give credence to the idea that if one can simply be positive enough all the time and keep up one's spirits, one could beat cancer primarily with one's mind. This mind-over-matter approach caused a great deal of grief for cancer patients who couldn't always be upbeat.

I think two messages can be taken from this study. The first is that persons who find it difficult to be combative, to maintain a fighting spirit all the time, don't have to feel the pressure of always being positive, which can remove their burden of guilt. The other message is that feeling helpless and hopeless may be a symptom of depression. Therefore, it's very important that doctors recommend treatment for depression, including counselling and perhaps anti-depressant medication to help improve the chances for survival—and at the very least help these patients improve their emotional well-being.

One well-wisher presented me a picture of a winter sunset—the sun is going down, pointing out the reality that a day is over. It always reminds me of forgiveness. What has been done or not done during that day—the good and the bad, the important and the unimportant—remains just the way it happened, or failed to happen. But when the sun returns again the next day, there is the possibility that things can be different. In accepting things just as they are and making the best of each day, we can create one of the most important foundations for health and recovery from illness. Conversely, one of the most damaging things is holding onto the past, holding onto guilt, regrets, resentments, old angers and old hurts.

Let us think we all live, metaphorically speaking, in a house that has windows facing in each direction—north, south, east, west. Yet we usually have a favourite window through which we view the world, let's say the one that shows us the territory to the north. Of course, we may sometimes look through another window, perhaps the one that faces east. But we tend to ignore the others. We may even forget they are there. So therapy, imagery techniques, and much of learning in general, it seems to me, are experiences that allow us to look through new windows. That doesn't mean that the view from the window or windows we've been using is wrong. But it does mean that sometimes we need a little help to look in a new direction and discover that life offers many more choices than we previously thought.

I always tell patients who come with diagnosed cancers to seek my guidance, "Don't deny the diagnosis; try to defy the verdict." Unfortunately, upon hearing the words of the all-knowing doctor, the patient naturally believes there is nothing to be done but accept his fate. It is true, of course, that perhaps nothing can change the course of the disease. After all, cancer is difficult to treat and is frequently fatal. However, from that moment on if the patient simply waits for the end, like a man on death row when his last appeal has been denied, he is not adopting the correct approach. In accepting the *sentence* handed down, he misses out on whatever joy life could grant him for whatever time he has left.

We all can know intuitively, if we sincerely try, about the role of hope and healing. We can feel deep in our bones and muscles a strength to carry on when we have hope that things will turn out for the best, if we just keep on. We also know the dread that pulls us down when we are sure we'll be defeated in trying to reach a goal. "What's the use?" the patient asks. Any life-challenging situation forces us to confront our most basic beliefs. A diagnosis of cancer is definitely one of those times. I once saw a visitor bringing a bunch of white lilies to a cancer patient in the hospital room. I asked him why had he chosen the white lilies. He answered that the purity of white lilies symbolises the quest for simplicity and peace of mind, something his friend needed most. What a thoughtful gift! I always want to tell my cancer patients to relax their bodies, expand their minds, increase pain tolerance, forgive themselves and others, embrace qualities of the human spirit, become aware of and connect with body's healing ability, uncover symbols of strength and courage and create harmony and wholeness in their lives. Most of the time I fail. May be after reading it you would do that to any one you come across suffering. □

9

Thoughtful contemplation of the human body evokes both admiration and alarm. Take the eye, for instance. The clear living tissue of the cornea curves just the right degree, the iris adjusts to brightness and the lens to distance, so that the optimal quantity of light focuses exactly on the surface of the retina. Admiration for such apparent perfection soon gives way, however, to alarm. Contrary to any sensible design, blood vessels and nerves traverse the inside of the retina, creating a blind spot at their point of exit.

The body is a bundle of such jarring contradictions. For each exquisite heart valve, we have a wisdom tooth. Strands of DNA direct the development of the 60 trillion cells that make up a human adult but then permit his or her steady deterioration and eventual death. Our immune system can identify and destroy a million kinds of foreign matter, yet many bacteria can still kill us. These contradictions make it appear as if evolution has built certain flaws and defects into the human body to ensure its mortality.

The concepts of evolutionary biology are just now being accepted in medical science. In contrast to explaining the causes of an individual's disease and seeking therapies to cure or relieve deleterious conditions, evolutionary biology asks why the body is designed in a way that makes us all vulnerable to problems like cancer, atherosclerosis, depression and choking. Unlike thousands of explanations for hundreds of diseases, evolutionary explanations for the body's flaws fall into surprisingly three categories. First, some discomforting conditions, such as pain, fever, cough, vomiting and anxiety, are actually neither diseases nor design defects but are rather evolved defences. Second, some circumstances, such as the ready availability of dietary fats, are so recent that natural selection has not yet had a chance to deal with them. And third, the body may fall victim to a trade-off between a trait's benefits and its costs; a textbook example is the sickle cell gene, which also protects against malaria. I feel it is important to discuss this new line of thought to put at rest some of the fears that always keep lurking in the mind about death and disease.

Let us begin with evolved defences. Perhaps the most obviously useful defence mechanism is coughing; people who cannot clear foreign matter from their lungs are likely to die from pneumonia. The capacity for pain is also certainly beneficial. The rare individuals who cannot feel pain fail even to experience discomfort from staying in the same position for long periods. Their unnatural stillness impairs blood supply to their joints, which then deteriorate. Such pain-free people usually die from tissue damage and infections by early adulthood. Cough or pain is usually interpreted as disease or trauma but is actually a part of the solution rather than the problem. These defensive capabilities, shaped by natural selection, are kept in reserve until needed.

Less widely recognised as defences are fever, nausea, vomiting, diarrhoea, anxiety, fatigue, sneezing and inflammation. Even some physicians remain unaware of fever's utility. No mere increase in metabolic rate, fever is a carefully regulated rise in the set point of the body's thermostat. The higher body temperature facilitates destruction of pathogens. A reduced level of iron in the blood is another misunderstood defence mechanism. People suffering from chronic infection often have decreased levels of blood iron. Although such low iron is sometimes blamed for the illness, it actually is a protective response: during infection, iron is sequestered in the liver, which prevents invading bacteria from getting adequate supplies of this vital element. Morning sickness has long been considered an unfortunate side-effect of pregnancy. The nausea, however, coincides with the period of rapid tissue differentiation of the foetus, when development is most vulnerable to interference by toxins. And nauseated women tend to restrict their intake of strong-tasting, potentially harmful substances.

Another common condition, anxiety, obviously originated as

a defence in dangerous situations by promoting escape and avoidance. Selection for genes promoting anxious behaviours implies that there should be people who experience too much anxiety, and indeed there are. There should also be hypo-phobic individuals who have insufficient anxiety, either because of genetic tendencies or anti-anxiety drugs. The exact nature and frequency of such a syndrome is an open question, as few people come to psychiatrists complaining of insufficient apprehension. But if sought, the pathologically non-anxious may be found in emergency rooms, jails and unemployment lines.

The utility of common and unpleasant conditions such as diarrhoea, fever and anxiety is not intuitive. If natural selection shapes the mechanisms that regulate defensive responses, how can people get away by using drugs to block these defences without doing their bodies obvious harm? Part of the answer is that we in fact, sometimes do ourselves a disservice by disrupting defences.

Studies on diarrhoea caused by infection revealed that people who took anti-diarrhoea drugs stayed sick longer and were more likely to have complications than those who took a placebo. In another study, it was found that well-intentioned attempts to correct perceived iron deficiencies had led to increases in infectious diseases, especially amoebiasis. Although the iron in most oral supplements is unlikely to make much difference in otherwise healthy people with everyday infections, it can severely harm those who are infected and malnourished. Such people cannot make enough protein to bind the iron, leaving it free for use by infectious agents.

On the morning-sickness front, an anti-nausea drug was recently blamed for birth defects. It appears that no consideration was given to the possibility that the drug itself might be harmless to the foetus but could still be associated with birth defects, by interfering with the mother's defensive nausea.

Another obstacle to perceiving the benefits of defences arises from the observation that many individuals regularly experience seemingly worthless reactions of anxiety, pain, fever, diarrhoea or nausea. The explanation requires an analysis of the regulation of defensive responses in terms of signal-detection theory. A circulating toxin may come from something in the stomach. An organism can expel it by vomiting, but only at a price. The cost of a false alarm—vomiting when no toxin is truly present—is only a few calories. But the penalty for a single missed authentic alarm—failure to vomit when confronted with a toxin—may be death.

Natural selection, therefore, tends to shape regulation mechanisms with hair triggers, following what we call the smoke-detector principle. A smoke alarm that reliably wakes a sleeping family in the event of any fire will necessarily give a false alarm every time the toast burns. The price of the human body's numerous *smoke alarms* is suffering that is completely normal but in most instances unnecessary. This principle also explains why the blocking of defences is so often free of tragic consequences. Because most defensive reactions occur in response to insignificant threats, interference is usually harmless; the vast majority of alarms that are stopped by removing the battery from the smoke alarm are false ones, so this strategy may seem reasonable. Until, that is, a real fire occurs.

Making rounds in any modern hospital provides sad testimony to the diseases humanity has brought on itself. Heart attacks, for example, result mainly from atherosclerosis, a problem that became widespread only in this century. Heart disease was rare among hunter-gatherers. Epidemiological research furnishes information that should help us prevent heart attacks: limit fat intake, eat lots of vegetables and exercise hard each day. But hamburger chains proliferate, diet foods languish on the shelves and exercise machines serve as expensive clothing hangers in the houses of the rich and famous. The proportion of overweight Indians is one fourth and rising. We all know what is good for us. Why do so many of us continue to make unhealthy choices?

Our poor decisions about diet and exercise are made by brains shaped to cope with an environment substantially different from the one our species now inhabits. On the African *savanna,* where the modern human design was fine-tuned, fat, salt and sugar were scarce and precious. Individuals who had a tendency to consume large amounts of fat when given the rare opportunity had a selective advantage. They were more likely to survive famines that killed their thinner companions. And we, their descendants, still carry those urges for foodstuffs that today are anything but scarce. These evolved desires—whipped up by advertisements from competing food corporations that themselves survive by selling us more of whatever we want to buy—easily defeat our intellect and willpower. How ironic that humanity worked for centuries to create an environment that is almost literally flowing with milk and honey, only to see our success responsible for much modern disease and untimely death.

Increasingly, people also have easy access to many kinds of drugs, especially alcohol and tobacco that are responsible for a huge proportion of diseases, healthcare costs and premature death. Although individuals have always used psychoactive substances, widespread problems materialised only following another environmental novelty: the ready availability of concentrated drugs and new, direct routes of administration, especially injection. Most of these substances, including nicotine, cocaine and opium, are products of natural selection that evolved to protect plants from insects. Because humans share a common evolutionary heritage with insects, many of these substances also affect our nervous system.

This perspective suggests that it is not just defective individuals or disordered societies that are vulnerable to the dangers of psychoactive drugs; all of us are susceptible because drugs and our biochemistry have a long history of interaction. Understanding the details of that interaction, which is the focus of much current research from both a proximate and evolutionary perspective, may well lead to better treatments for addiction.

The relatively recent and rapid increase in breast cancer must be the result in large part of changing environments and ways of life, with only a few cases resulting solely from genetic abnormalities. Project *TULASI,* a cancer screening exercise we undertook in villages, reveals that the rate of breast cancer in tribal women is only a tiny fraction of that in the urban women. It appears that the amount of time between menarche and first pregnancy is a crucial risk factor, as is the related issue of total lifetime number of menstrual cycles. In hunter-gatherers, menarche occurs about age 15 or later, followed within a few years by pregnancy and two or three years of nursing, then by another pregnancy soon after. Only between the end of nursing and the next pregnancy will the woman menstruate and thus experience high levels of hormones that may adversely affect breast cells.

In urban societies, in contrast, menarche occurs at age 12 or 13—probably at least in part because of a fat intake sufficient to allow an extremely young woman to nourish a foetus—and the first pregnancy may be decades later or never. A tribal female may have a total of 150 menstrual cycles, whereas the average woman in cities has 400 or more. The idea is not to suggest that women should become pregnant in their teens to prevent breast cancer later but to examine if early administration of a burst of hormones to simulate pregnancy may reduce the risk. Compromise is inherent in every adaptation. Arm bones three times their current thickness would almost never break, but homo sapiens would be lumbering creatures on a never-ending quest for calcium. More sensitive ears might sometimes be useful, but we would be distracted by the noise of air molecules banging into our eardrums.

Such trade-offs also exist at the genetic level. If a mutation offers a net reproductive advantage, it will tend to increase in frequency in a population even if it causes vulnerability to disease. People with two copies of the sickle cell gene, for example suffer terrible pain and die young. People with two copies of the "normal" gene are at high risk of death from malaria. But individuals with one of each are protected from both malaria and sickle cell disease. Where malaria is prevalent, such people are fitter, in the Darwinian sense than members of either other group. So even though the sickle cell gene causes disease, it is selected for where malaria persists. Which is the *healthy allele* in this environment? The question has no answer. There is no one normal human genome—there are only genes.

Many other genes that cause disease must also have offered benefits, at least in some environments, or they would not be so common. Because cystic fibrosis (CF) kills one out of 2,500 Caucasians, the responsible genes would appear to be at great risk of being eliminated from the gene pool. And yet they endure. For years, researchers mused that the CF gene, like the sickle cell gene, probably conferred some advantage. Having one copy of the CF gene appears to decrease the chances of the bearer acquring a typhoid fever infection, which once had a 15 per cent mortality.

Ageing may be the ultimate example of a genetic trade-off. It is suggested that genes that cause ageing and eventual death could nonetheless be selected for if they gave an advantage in youth, when the force of selection is stronger. For instance, a hypothetical gene which governs calcium metabolism and helps bones heal quickly but which also causes the steady deposition of calcium in arterial walls killing some older people might well be selected. The influence of such pleiotropic genes (those having multiple effects) has been seen in fruit flies and flour beetles, but no specific example has yet been found in humans. Gout, however, is of particular interest, because it arises when a potent antioxidant, uric icid, forms crystals that precipitate out of fluid in joints. Antioxidants have anti-ageing effects, and plasma levels of uric acid in different species of primates are closely correlated with average adult life span. Perhaps high levels of uric acid benefit most humans by slowing tissue ageing, while a few pay the price with gout.

Other examples are more likely to contribute to more rapid ageing. For instance, strong immune defences protect us from infection but also inflict continuous, low-level tissue damage. It is also possible, of course, that most genes that cause ageing have no benefit at any age—they simply never decreased reproductive fitness enough in the natural environment to be selected against. Nevertheless, over the next decade research will surely identify specific genes that accelerate senescence, and researchers will soon thereafter gain the means to interfere with their actions or even change them. Before we tinker, however, we should determine whether these actions have benefits early in life.

Because evolution can take place only in the direction of time's arrow, an organism's design is constrained by structures already in place. As I mentioned earlier, the vertebrate eye is arranged backward. The squid eye, in contrast, is free from this defect, with vessels and nerves running on the outside, penetrating where necessary and pinning down the retina so that it cannot detach. The human eye's flaw results from simple bad luck; hundreds of millions of years ago, the layer of cells that happened to become sensitive to light in our ancestors was positioned differently from the corresponding layer in ancestors of squids. The two designs evolved along separate tracks, and there is no going back.

Such path dependence also explains why the simple act of swallowing can be life-threatening. Our respiratory and food passages intersect because in an early lungfish ancestor the air opening for breathing at the surface was understandably located at the top of the snout and led into a common space shared by the food passageway. Because natural selection cannot start from scratch, humans are stuck with the possibility that food will clog the opening to our lungs.

The path of natural selection can even lead to a potentially fatal cul-de-sac, as in the case of the appendix, that vestige of a cavity that our ancestors employed in digestion. Because it no longer performs that function, and as it can kill when infected, the expectation might be that natural selection would have eliminated it. The reality is more complex. Appendicitis results when inflammation causes swelling, which compresses the artery supplying blood to the appendix. Blood flow protects against bacterial growth, so any reduction aids infection, which creates more swelling. If the blood supply is cut off completely, bacteria have free rein until the appendix bursts. A slender appendix is especially susceptible to this chain of events, so appendicitis may, paradoxically, apply the selective pressure that maintains a large appendix. Far from arguing that everything in the body is perfect, an evolutionary analysis reveals that we live with some very unfortunate legacies and that some vulnerabilities may even be actively maintained by the force of natural selection.

As most diseases decrease fitness, so it would seem that natural selection could explain only health, not disease. An evolutionary approach makes sense only when the object of explanation is changed from diseases to the traits that make us vulnerable to diseases. The assumption that natural selection maximises health also is incorrect—selection maximises the reproductive success of genes. Those genes that make bodies having superior reproductive success will become more common, even if they compromise the individual's health in the end. The evolutionary viewpoint provides a deep connection between the states of disease and normal functioning and can integrate disparate avenues of medical research as well as suggest fresh and important areas of inquiry. Its utility and power will ultimately lead to recognition of evolutionary biology as a basic medical science.

The systematic application of evolutionary biology to medicine is a new enterprise. Like biochemistry at the beginning of this century, evolutionary medicine very likely will need to develop in several incubators before it can prove its power and utility. If it must progress only from the work of scholars without funding to gather data to test their ideas, it will take decades for the field to mature. Departments of evolutionary biology in medical schools would accelerate the process, but for the most part they do not yet exist. If funding agencies had review panels with evolutionary expertise, research would develop faster, but such panels remain to be created. I expect that they will be.

Ever since antibiotics became widely available in the 1940s, they have been hailed as miracle drugs—magic bullets to eliminate bacteria without doing much harm to the cells of treated individuals. Yet with each passing decade, bacteria that defy not only single but multiple antibiotics—and, therefore, are extremely difficult to control—have become increasingly common. How did we end up in this worrisome and worsening, situation? Several interacting processes are at fault. Analyses of them point to a number of actions that could help reverse the trend, if individuals, businesses and governments around the world can find the will to implement them.

One component of the solution is recognising that bacteria are a natural, and needed, part of life. Bacteria, which are microscopic, single-cell entities, abound on inanimate surfaces and on parts of the body that make contact with the outer world, including the skin, the mucous membranes and the lining of the intestinal tract. Most live blamelessly. In fact, they often protect us from disease, because they compete with, and thus limit the proliferation of, pathogenic bacteria—the minority of species that can multiply aggressively (into the millions) and damage tissues or otherwise cause illness. The benign competitors can be important allies in the fight against antibiotic-resistant pathogens.

People should also realise that although antibiotics are needed to control bacterial infections, they can have broad, undesirable effects on microbial ecology. That is, they can produce long-lasting change in the kinds and proportions of bacteria—and the mix of antibiotic-resistant and antibiotic-susceptible types—not only in the treated individual but also in the environment and society at large. The compounds should thus be used only when they are truly needed, and they should not be administered for viral infections, over which they have no power. Although many factors can influence whether bacteria in a person or in a community will become insensitive to an antibiotic, the two main forces are the prevalence of resistance genes (which give rise to proteins that shield bacteria from an antibiotic's effects) and the extent of antibiotic use. If the collective bacterial flora in a community have no genes conferring resistance to a given antibiotic, the antibiotic will successfully eliminate infection caused by any of the bacterial species in the collection. On the other hand, if the flora possess resistance genes and the community uses the drug persistently, bacteria able to defy eradication by the compound will emerge and multiply.

Antibiotic-resistant pathogens are not more virulent than susceptible ones: the same numbers of resistant and susceptible bacterial cells are required to produce disease. But the resistant forms are harder to destroy. Using more of the drug can often eliminate those that are slightly insensitive to an antibiotic, those that are highly resistant require other therapies. To understand how resistance genes enable bacteria to survive an attack by an antibiotic, it helps to know exactly what antibiotics are and how they harm bacteria. Strictly speaking, the compounds are defined as natural substances (made by living organisms) that inhibit the growth or proliferation of bacteria or kill them directly. In practice, though, most commercial antibiotics have been chemically altered in the laboratory to improve their potency or to increase the range of species they affect.

Whatever they're antibiotics, by inhibiting bacterial growth, give a host's immune defences a chance to outflank the bugs that remain. The drugs typically retard bacterial proliferation by entering the microbes and interfering with the production of components needed to form new bacterial cells. For instance, the antibiotic tetracycline binds to ribosomes (internal structures that make new proteins) and, in so doing, impairs protein manufacture; penicillin and vancomycin impede proper synthesis of the bacterial cell wall.

Certain resistance genes ward off destruction by giving rise to enzymes that degrade antibiotics or that chemically modify, and so inactivate, the drugs. Alternatively, some resistance genes cause bacteria to alter or replace molecules that are normally bound by antibiotic changes that essentially eliminate the drug's targets in bacterial cells. Bacteria might also eliminate entry ports for the drugs or, more effectively, may manufacture pumps that export antibiotics before the medicines have a chance to find their intracellular targets.

Bacteria can acquire resistance genes through a few routes. Many inherit the genes from their forerunners. Other times, genetic mutations, which occur readily in bacteria, will spontaneously produce a new resistance trait or will strengthen an existing one. And frequently, bacteria will gain a defence against an antibiotic by taking up resistance genes from other bacterial cells in the vicinity. Indeed, the exchange of genes is so pervasive that the entire bacterial world can be thought of as one huge multi-cellular organism in which the cells interchange their genes with ease.

Bacteria have evolved several ways to share their resistance traits with one another. Resistance genes commonly are carried on plasmids, tiny loops of DNA that can help bacteria survive various hazards in the environment. But the genes may also occur on the bacterial chromosome, the larger DNA molecule that stores the genes needed for the reproduction and routine maintenance of a bacterial cell.

Often one bacterium will pass resistance traits to others by giving them a useful plasmid. Resistance genes can also be transferred by viruses that occasionally extract a gene from one bacterial cell and inject it into a different one. In addition, after a bacterium dies and releases its contents into the environment, another will occasionally take up a liberated gene for itself.

In the last two situations, the gene will survive and provide protection from an antibiotic only if integrated stable into a plasmid or chromosome. Such integration occurs frequently, though, because resistance genes are often embedded in small units of DNA, called *transposons,* that readily hop into other DNA molecules. In a regrettable twist of fate for human beings, many bacteria play host to specialised *transposons,* termed *integrons,* that are like flypaper in their propensity for capturing new genes. These *integrons* can consist of several different resistance genes, which are passed to other bacteria as whole regiments of antibiotic-defying guerrillas.

Many bacteria possessed resistance genes even before commercial antibiotics came into use. Scientists do not know exactly why these genes evolved and were maintained. A logical argument holds that natural antibiotics were initially elaborated as a result of chance genetic mutations. Then the compounds, which turned out to eliminate competitors, enabled the manufacturers to survive and proliferate—if they were also lucky enough to possess genes that protected them from their own chemical weapons. Later, these protective genes found their way into other species, some of which were pathogenic. Regardless of how bacteria acquire resistance genes today, commercial antibiotics can promote the survival and ropagation of antibiotic-resistant strains. In other words, by encouraging the growth of resistant pathogens, an antibiotic can actually contribute to its own undoing.

Promoting resistance in known pathogens is not the only self-defeating activity of antibiotics. When the medicines attack disease-causing bacteria, they also affect benign bacteria—innocent bystanders—in their path. They eliminate drug-susceptible bystanders that could otherwise limit the expansion of pathogens, and they simultaneously encourage the growth of resistant bystanders. Propagation of these resistant, non-pathogenic bacteria increases the reservoir of resistance traits in the bacterial population as a whole and raises the odds that such traits will spread to pathogens. In addition, sometimes the growing populations of bystanders themselves become agents of disease.

Widespread use of cephalosporin antibiotics, for example, has promoted the proliferation of the once benign intestinal bacterium *E. faecalis,* which is naturally resistant to those drugs. In most people, the immune system is able to check the growth of even multi drug-resistant E. *faecalis,* so that it does not produce illness. But in hospitalised patients with compromised imunity, the enterococcus can spread to the heart valves and other organs and establish deadly systemic disease. The bystander effect has also enabled multidrug-resistant strains of *Acinetobacter* and *Xanthomonas* to emerge and become agents of potentially fatal blood-borne infections in hospitalised patients. These formerly innocuous microbes were virtually unheard of just five years ago. Death has nothing terrible which life had not made so.

□

10

Throughout the book I have discussed death and disease. But what is Life? Is it a philosophical question? My answer is a firm no. Life is very real, very physical and very substantial. After spending a lifetime in medical profession, my thesis would be a theory of people living within the philosophical framework of ecology and spirituality. The understanding of pattern in which we all live is crucial to the scientific understanding of the human life, specially for those who are in the medical profession. I have come to believe that to comprehend the essence of human life, it is essential to understand pattern (or form, order, quality) that binds the structure (or substance, matter, quantity). The pattern of organisation of human body can, therefore, be understood as the configuration of relationships among the body's components that determine the essential characteristics of body's functions. In this concluding chapter, I will attempt to provide emerging knowledge of health, which is quite different from what has so far been considered as fact.

Let us look at something very simple, like a bicycle. In order for something to be called a bicycle, there must be a number of functional relationships between components known as frame, pedals, handlebars, wheels, chain, sprocket, etc. Unless these components are configured into a functional relationship the assembly will not become a system and be called a bicycle. The availability of all of those relationships must be present to give the system the essential characteristics of a bicycle. The structure of the bicycle is the physical embodiment of its pattern of organisation in terms of components of specific shapes, made of specific materials. The same pattern of "bicycle" can be embodied in many different structures. The handlebars will be shaped differently for a touring bike, a racing bike, or a mountain bike; the frame may be heavy and solid or light and delicate; the tyres may be narrow or wide, tubes or solid rubber. All these combinations and many more will easily be recognised as different embodiments of the same pattern of relationships that define a bicycle.

In a machine such as a bicycle the parts have been designed, manufactured and then put together to form a structure with fixed components. In a living system, by contrast, the components change continually. There is a ceaseless flux of matter through a living organism. Each cell continually synthesises and dissolves structures and eliminates waste products. Tissues and organs replace their cells in continual cycles. There is growth, development and evolution. Thus from the very beginning of biology, the understanding of living structure has been inseparable from the understanding of metabolic and developmental processes.

This striking property of living systems suggests process as a third criterion for a comprehensive description of the nature of life. The process of life is the activity involved in the continual embodiment of the system's pattern of organisation. Thus the process criterion is the link between pattern and structure. In the case of the bicycle, the pattern of organisation is represented by the design sketches that are used to build the bicycle, the structure is a specific physical bicycle, and the link between pattern and structure is in the mind of the designer. In the case of a living organism, however, the pattern of organisation is always embodied in the organisation's structure, and the link between pattern and structure lies in the process of continual embodiment. All the three criteria are totally interdependent. In a nutshell, I identify self-making, as the pattern of life, disintegration of the existing as the structure of living system, and cognition as the process of life.

By self-making as the pattern of life I mean a network in which the function of each component is to participate in the production or transformation of other components in the network. In this way, the network continually makes itself. It is produced by its components and in turn produces those components—*omnis cellula e cellula*—"every cell originates from a previously existing cell."

The simplest living system we know is a cell. I have discussed cells in Chapter 3. But let me again discuss them, this time as a network. Let us take a typical plant cell. It consists of a membrane which encloses the cell fluid *(cytoplasm* in Greek). The fluid is rich molecular soup of the chemical elements out of which the cell builds its structures. Suspended in the cell fluid we find the cell nucleus, a large number of tiny production centres (ribosome; a composite of ribonucleic acid—RNA—and mirosome—microscopic body—denoting a tiny granule containing RNA) where the main structural building-blocks are produced, and several specialised parts, called *organelles,* which are analogous to body organs. The most important of these *organelles* are the storage sacs (called Golgi apparatus after the Italian physician Camillo Golgi), recycling centres *(lysosome* or dissolving body), powerhouses *(mitochondrion* or thread like granule), and solar stations *(cytoplast* or green leaf). Like the cell as a whole, the nucleus and the *organelles* are surrounded by semi-permeable membranes that select what comes in and what goes out. The cell membrane, in particular, takes in food and dissipates waste.

The cell nucleus contains the generic material, i.e. the DNA molecules carrying the genetic information, and the RNA molecules, which are made by the DNA to deliver instructions to the production centres. The nucleus also contains a smaller 'mini nucleus' *(nucleolus* or small nucleus), where the production centres are made before being distributed throughout the cell The production centres are granular bodies in which the cell's proteins are produced. These include structural proteins as well as enzymes, the catalysts that promote all cellular processes. There are about 500,000 production centres in each cell,

The storage sacs are stacks of flat pouches, somewhat like a pile of *roties,* where various cellular products are stored and then labelled, packaged and sent on to their destinations. The recycling centres are *organelles* containing enzymes for digesting food, damaged cell components and various unused molecules. The broken-down elements are then recycled and used for building new cell components. The powerhouses carry out the cellular respiration, i.e. they use oxygen to break down organic molecules into carbon dioxide and water. This releases energy that is locked up in special energy carriers. These energy carriers are complex molecular compounds that travel to the other parts of the cell to supply energy for all cellular processes known collectively as 'cell metabolism'. The energy carriers serve as the cell's main energy units, not unlike cash in the human economy.

I have opted to include this information here to emphasise that in order to give even a rough idea of cellular organisation, the description of the cell's components has to be quite elaborate. The complexity increases dramatically when we try to picture how these cell components are inter-linked in a vast network, involving thousands of metabolic processes. The enzymes alone form an intricate network of catalytic reactions, promoting all metabolic processes, and the energy carriers from a corresponding energy network to fuel them.

Let me take just one single loop to illustrate the nature of this network. The DNA in the cell nucleus produces RNA molecules, which contain instructions for the production of proteins, including enzymes. Among these is a group of special enzymes that can recognise, remove and replace damaged sections of DNA. Each component in the network helps produce or transform other components, turning it self-making. The DNA produces the RNA, the RNA specifies the enzymes and the enzymes repair the DNA.

To complete the picture, we would have to add the building blocks from which DNA, RNA and enzymes are made: the energy carriers fuelling each of the processes, the generation of the energy in the powerhouses from broken-down sugars; and the production of the sugars by photosynthesis in the solar stations, etc. With each addition to the network we would see that the new components, too, help produce and transform other components, and thus the self-making nature of the entire network would become even more apparent.

The case of the cell membrane is especially interesting. It is a boundary of the cell, formed by some of the cell's components, which encloses the network of metabolic processes and thus limits their extension. At the same time, the membrane participates in the network by selecting the raw material for the production processes through special filters and by dissipating waste into the outside environment. Thus, the self-making network creates its own boundary, which defines the cell as a distinct system while being an active part of the network.

Since all components of a self-making network are produced by other components in the network, the entire system is organisationally closed, even though it is open with regard to the flow of energy and matter. This organisational closure implies that a living system is self-organising in the sense that its order and behaviour are not imposed by the environment but are established by the system itself. In other words, life is autonomous. Also, self-making networks must continually regenerate themselves to maintain their organisation. This, of course, is a well-known characteristic of life.

I will conclude this brief ingraining by describing mind as a process—the very process of life. Mind is the essence of being alive. "I am because I am." The organising activity of living systems, at all levels of life, is mental activity. Mental process is immanent in matter at all levels of life. A set of criteria has emerged that systems have to satisfy for mind to occur—learning, memory, and decision making, etc. The brain is a specific structure through which this process operates. The human nervous system does not process any information, but interacts with the environment by continually modulating its structures. Human intelligence, human memory and human decisions are never completely rational but are always coloured by emotions.

All cell types in the body—skin, liver, heart, brain, and so on—in spite of their very different shapes and functions, contain roughly the same genetic instructions. The cell types differ from one another not because they contain different genes, but because the genes that are active in them differ. In other words, the structure of the genetic material is the same in all cells, but the pattern of genetic activity is different. The 30,000 genes in humans express themselves in about 254 different cell types. All these genes were acquired by children from their parents and passed on to their children. This is the eternity of life.

The science of medicine, unfortunately is still based on the notion of the body as a machine, of disease as the consequence of breakdown of the machine, and of the doctor's task as repair of the machine. By concentrating on smaller and smaller fragments of the body, modern medicine often loses sight of the patient as a human being, and by reducing health to mechanical functioning, it is no longer able to deal with the phenomenon of healing. Although every practising physician knows that healing is an essential aspect of all medicine, the phenomenon is considered outside the scientific framework; the term 'healer' is viewed with suspicion, and the concepts of health and healing are generally not discussed in our medical colleges. I believe that it is our duty as physicians to estimate probabilities and to discipline expectations; but leading away from probabilities there are paths of possibility, towards which it is also our duty to hold aloft hope and healing.

The healing of wounds and the healing of illnesses essentially involves a complex interplay among the physical, psychological, social and environmental aspects of the human condition. To reincorporate the notion of healing into the theory and practice of medicine, medical science will have to transcend it's narrow view of health and illness. This does not mean that it will have to be less scientific. On the contrary, by broadening its conceptual basis it will become more consistent with recent developments in modern science.

Health and the phenomenon of healing have meant different things in different ages. The concept of health, like the concept of life, cannot be defined precisely, and in fact, the two are closely related. The definition of health given by the World Health Organisation in the preamble of its charter needs reading: "Health is a state of complete physical, mental and social well-being and not merely the absence of disease or infirmity." Though I find the definition somewhat unrealistic, it conveys the holistic nature of health, which has to be grasped if we are to understand the phenomenon of healing.

In Indian societies, through the ages healing has been practised by healers—*vaidyas, sidhhas, hakims,* folk healers—who are guided by traditional wisdom that sees illness as a disorder of the whole person, involving not only the patient's body but his mind; his self-image, his dependence on the physical and social environment, as well as his relation to the cosmos and the deities. These healers, who still treat a majority of one billion Indians, follow many different approaches, which are holistic to different degrees, and they use a wide variety of therapeutic techniques. They are quite different from one another and yet what they have in common is that they never restrict themselves to purely physical phenomena. Through rituals and ceremonies, avoidance of this or that food intake, they attempt to influence the patient's mind, relieving the apprehension that is always a significant component of illness and helping the patient to stimulate self-making forces—the natural healing powers—that all living organisms possess.

In modern scientific terms I can say that the healing process represents the coordinated response of the integrated organism to stressful environmental influences. Even Western medicine emerged from a large reservoir of folk healing and subsequently spread to the rest of the world including India. Most of our societies show a pluralism of medical systems and medical beliefs, with no sharp dividing lines between one system and another. The *Ayurveda* is based on a written tradition, using empirical knowledge and is practised by a professional elite. So are *Unani, Sidhha* and Homeopathy to a varying degree. The approach of all of them is holistic, if not always in actual practice, then at least in theory. In addition to these systems, we have regional and local popular medicine—beliefs and practices used within family, or a community, which are passed on by word of mouth and practised by one and all. Since the Indian ethos relates the act of healing to mother, the practice of popular medicine is mainly the prerogative of women in the families. Dr. Abdul Kalam writes about his mother in *Wings of Fire:*

Your caring hands, tenderly removing the pain
Your love, your care, your faith gave me strength
To face the world without fear and with His strength.

The rise of the modern scientific medicine—I would not term as Western Medicine—began in the nineteenth century with the great advances made in biology but the real bang came from Louis Pasteur who demonstrated correlation between bacteria and disease. His doctrine that specific diseases are caused by specific microbes was swiftly accepted by medical profession. The great genius of Pasteur showed a strong ecological awareness. In fact he started from the point that the healthy body exhibits a striking resistance to many types of microbes. He knew very well that every human organism acts as host to a multitude of bacteria, and he pointed out that these can cause damage only when the body is weakened. Thus, in Pasteur's view, successful therapy will often depend on the physician's ability to restore the physiological conditions favourable to natural resistance. Pasteur boldly suggested that mental states affect resistance to infection. It is an irony that intuitively anticipated mind-body approach of the founder of microbiology to therapy is still suspect in medical establishments.

Twentieth century medicine is characterised by the understanding of life at the molecular level and the rise of medical technology to a level where almost every organ is *seen* in its minutest detail and genes are *picked* from nucleus of the cells. In the long rise of scientific medicine, physicians have gained fascinating insights into the intimate mechanisms of the human body and have developed their technologies to an impressive degree of complexity and sophistication. In spite of these great advances in medical science we are now witnessing a profound crisis in healthcare in Europe and North America. Many reasons are given for the widespread dissatisfaction with medical institutions. They include inaccessibility of services, lack of sympathy and care and malpractice, but the central theme of all criticism is the striking disproportion between the cost and effectiveness of modern medicine. Despite a staggering increase in health costs over the past four decades, and amid continuing claims of scientific and technological excellence by the medical profession, the health of American population does not seem to have improved significantly.

The relation between medicine and health is difficult to assess because most health statistics use the narrow definition of health as absence of disease. A meaningful assessment would deal with both the health of the individual and the health of the society; it would have to include mental illness and social pathologies. Such a comprehensive view would show that, although medicine has contributed to the elimination of certain diseases, this has definitely not restored health. Newer diseases have arrived, some out of use and abuse of newer drugs, some from newer lifestyles. In contemporary Western societies, psychological and social pathologies have already become major problems of public health. According to some surveys, as many as 25 per cent of American population is sufficiently troubled psychologically to be seriously handicapped and in need of therapeutic attention. At the same time there has been an alarming rise in alcoholism, violent crimes, accidents and suicides—all symptoms of social ill health. Similarly, the current serious health problems of children in Europe have to be seen as indicators of social illness, along with the rise in crime and political terrorism. The Kashmir Valley has seen more deaths in the last one decade in spite of its most favourable climate for recovery and convalescence. On healthcare front, we may not have achieved much but we didn't lose much either. This is a big lesson for anybody who wishes to learn.

In discussing the relation between medicine and health, one also has to realise that there is a whole spectrum of medicine, from general practice to emergency medicine and surgery to psychiatry. In some of these areas scientific medicine has been highly successful whereas in others it has proven to be rather ineffective. The great success of emergency medicine in dealing with accidents, acute infections and premature births is well known. Almost everyone knows somebody whose life has been saved, or whose pain and discomfort have been dramatically reduced by medical intervention. Indeed, medical technologies are superb in dealing with these emergencies. Although such medical care can be decisive in individual cases, it does not seem to make a significant difference for the health of population as a whole. The great publicity given to such spectacular medical procedures as open-heart surgery and organ transplants tend to make us forget that many of these patients would not have been hospitalised in the first place if preventive measures had not been severely neglected.

A dramatic development in the history of public health, for which modern medicine is usually given credit and an Indian looks at America and Europe with awe, has been the elimination of infectious diseases. Diseases like tuberculosis, cholera and typhoid are still a constant threat in this part of the world whereas they have almost completely disappeared in the developed countries, and the very rare occurrences can easily be controlled with antibodies. The fact that this dramatic change has taken place more or less simultaneously with the rise of modern scientific medicine has led to the widespread belief that it was brought about by the achievements of medical science. This belief, although shared by most doctors, is quite erroneous. Studies of the history of disease patterns have shown conclusively that the contribution of medical intervention to the decline of the infectious diseases has been much smaller than is generally believed.

The study of disease pattern in post-independence India will demonstrate to anyone that mortality has come down in all those pockets where people are fed well, lived cleanly and have smaller families. The critical role of nutrition in strengthening the response of the organism to infectious diseases is now well established the world over and is consistent with our own experience. And yet we keep opening hospitals showcasing the latest gadgets and wizardry at a great cost to the helpless patients. No one says the obvious that bad health originates from poverty, malnutrition and filth. There is no public movement for this public problem, no public campaign to combat these conditions. Nobody talks about technologies to provide purified water, safe milk and improved food hygiene—all extremely efficient in controlling the infectious diseases.

Let me tell in the simplest of words that the health of human beings is predominantly determined not by medical intervention but by their behaviour, their food and the nature of their environment. Since these variables differ from culture to culture, communities to communities, families to families, some fall sick and some do not. Then there are illnesses which are associated not with poverty and deficient living conditions but, on the contrary, with affluence and technological complexity. These are the chronic and degenerative diseases—heart disease, cancer, diabetes—that have aptly been called 'diseases of civilisation,' since they are closely related to the stressful attitudes, rich diet, sedentary living and environmental pollution all characteristics of modern life. There is no big secret. It's so obvious, plain and simple. We boil at different degrees.

Because of their difficulties in dealing with degenerative diseases, physicians often seem to resign themselves to accepting these diseases as inevitable consequences of 'wear and tear' for which there is no cure. By contrast, the patients are becoming increasingly dissatisfied with super speciality hospital healthcare, noticing painfully that it has generated exorbitant costs without significantly improving their health. In another social tragedy, instead of minding the basics of healthy living, they are turning to pseudo-therapies like magnetic healing, touch healing, auras and what not.

The causes of our health crisis are manifold. They can be found both within and without medical science and are inextricably linked to the larger social and cultural crisis. Still, an increasing number of people, both within and outside the medical field, perceive the shortcomings of the current healthcare system as being rooted in the conceptual framework that supports medical theory and practice, and have come to believe that the crisis will persist till this framework is modified. So I think it will be most appropriate for me to conclude my story with a conceptual springboard on which Indian healthcare system can launch itself in the 21st century.

Doctors practise medicine in many different ways with different personalities, attitudes and beliefs. Some family physicians are very caring and others care very little. There are surgeons who are highly spiritual and practise their art with a profound reverence for the human condition, and there are others who are cynical and profit-motivated. There are very touching experiences in hospitals, and there are others that are outrageously inhuman and degrading. In spite of this wide variety, however, one general belief system underlines current medical education and research and institutional healthcare. This belief system is based on the conceptual separation of mind and body.

This division has split the profession into two separate camps with very little communication between them. Physicians are concerned with the treatment of the body, psychiatrists and psychologists with the healing of the mind. The gap between the two groups has been a severe handicap in the understanding of most major diseases, because it has prevented medical researchers from studying the roles of stress and of emotional states in the development of illness. Stress has only very recently been recognised as a significant source of a wide range of disorders, and the link between emotional states and illness, although known throughout the ages, still receives little attention from the medical profession. Cancer studies are typical. The connection between emotional states and cancer has been well known for over 100 years. Substantial psychological literature is available reporting evidence but very few physicians would consider this knowledge and integrate psychological aspects into their treatment regimes. A person's psychological state may or may not be relevant in the generation of illness but I can say from my experience that it is crucial in the process of healing. The patient's psychological response to the physician is an important part, perhaps the most important part, of every therapy. To induce peace of mind and confidence in the healing process has always been a major purpose of the therapeutic encounter between doctor and patient, and it is well known among us doctors that this is usually done intuitively and has nothing to do with our training and clinical skills. Some doctors seem to make people well, while others, regardless of their expertise, have high rates of complications. The art of healing can't be scientifically quantified.

As I tried to explain earlier, there are beneficial aspects and potential meaning of illness. Every time we fall sick and undergo a natural recovery process we acquire immunity from a potential life threat and in fact grow stronger. Viewing disease as an enemy and trying to conquer it with vengeance and virility is almost foolish. Such a narrow point of view fails to comprehend the subtle psychological and spiritual aspects of illness. Siddhartha Gautam has defined suffering as an eternal truth. Complete freedom from disease and struggle is almost totally incompatible with the living process.

The ultimate existential issue is, of course, death—and, like all other philosophical and existential questions, the matter of death is avoided as much as possible. Because of the lack of spirituality that has become the characteristic of our modern materialistic society we seem to be trying to defy death. The distinction between a good death and a poor life is not understood even by the best of doctors. Whereas in the past, one of the most important roles of a good doctor was to provide comfort and support for dying patients and their families, physicians and other health professionals today are no longer trained to deal with the dying. They find it extremely difficult to cope with the phenomenon of death in a meaningful way. They tend to see death as a failure. The fact that it is perfectly possible to die in good health seems to have been forgotten by the medical profession. The story of Yaksha asking Dharmaraja about the most comical aspect of human nature and his answer, that man lives in delusion of immortality while seeing death everywhere around, seems to have been completely forgotten.

I have no intention of undermining the great role of medical technology and the highly sophisticated methods for removing or repairing various parts of the body, and even replacing the defunct ones by artificial constructs. This has alleviated the sufferings and discomforts of countless victims of illness and accidents, but unfortunately it has also helped to distort the views of health and healthcare held by the medical profession and the general public. The most terrible of lies is not that which is uttered but that which is lived.

The public image of the human organism—enforced by the content of television commercials—is that of a machine which is prone to constant failure unless supervised by doctors and supported by medication. A child needs particular toothpaste to keep his teeth intact. A student needs a particular food supplement to retain memory. A young woman must use a particular toiletry to manage her menstruation flow and an older one a particular cream to keep the skin from sagging. The notion of the organism's inherent healing power and tendency to stay healthy is not communicated, and trust in one's own organism is not promoted. Nor the relation between health and living habits is emphasised. In fact, bad habits are encouraged by promising false support from particular products. We are encouraged to assume that we can get away with all our habits and that certain products and doctors can fix anything, irrespective of our lifestyles.

It is intriguing and quite ironic that physicians themselves are the ones who suffer most from the mechanistic view of health by disregarding stressful circumstances in their lives. Whereas traditional healers were expected to be healthy people, keeping their body and soul in harmony and in tune with their environment, the typical attitudes and habits of doctors today are quite unhealthy and produce considerable illness. Many in my profession are overweight, indulge in alcohol, eat junk food, smoke, perform routine surgeries till 10 PM to earn more, and travel during nights to catch up with more and more patients. Their families suffer more social pathologies than any other occupational group.

Most doctors adopt unhealthy attitudes right at the beginning of medical college. They undergo a real cut-throat competition or alternatively cough up large sums of money to get into college. In college, their training is designed to be a highly stressful experience. The unhealthy value system that dominates our society has found some of its most extreme expressions in medical education. Like the modern business schools, medical colleges present high competitiveness as a virtue and emphasise an 'aggressive approach' to patient care. My friend, Dr. Abdul Kalam was very amused to find many of his defence related terms in my hospital. For example, patients are given 'shots' of antibiotics. A malignant tumour is said to 'invade' the body. Radiation therapy 'bombards' the tissues to 'kill' cancer cells, and chemotherapy is often likened to chemical warfare. It is not an exaggeration to say that medical education and practice perpetuate the attitudes and behaviour patterns of a value system that plays a significant role in causing many of these diseases medicine seeks to cure.

The emphasis on medical technology is out of proportion to its real utility. Exotic diagnostic tests have come to give a touch of class to the quality of treatment. In fact, medicine has not been able to prevent or cure any of our common major diseases over the past three celebrated decades of great advancements. We are, in a sense, stuck with technology, and we will stay stuck until we have more scientific knowledge to work with it. CTs are getting replaced with spiral CTs. MRIs are commonly used at great cost to patients. But there is hardly any new drug, new strategy, new treatment—be it cancer, or heart disease, neurological disorders.

Hard technology has turned hospitals into commercial facilities, where patients are charged by hours and minutes. While a patient gets radiation as an out-patient, hourly charges are billed for the duration he lies on the bed to receive IV fluid. When I started practice, the ratio of supporting personnel to doctors was about three to one; now it can be as high as ten to one. The diagnostic and therapeutic tools operated by this army of technicians are the result of recent advances in physics, chemistry, electronics, computer science and other related fields. They include computerised blood analysers and tomography scanners, machines for renal dialysis, cardiac pacemakers, equipment for radiation therapy, and many other machines that are not only highly sophisticated but also extremely expensive, some of them costing over a crore of rupees. As in other areas, the use of high technology in medicine is often unwarranted. The increasing dependence of medical care on complex technologies has accelerated the trend toward specialisation and the doctor's tendency to look at particular parts of the body, forgetting to deal with the patient as a whole person. The scanner assistant expects a child to finish drinking one litre of barium solution in 10 minutes. A radiation oncologist hardly inquires about the dryness of mouth in an elderly lady with the cancer of the tongue.

The excessive use of high technology in medical care is uneconomic and causes an unnecessary amount of pain and suffering. Accidents in hospitals now occur more frequently than in any other industry except perhaps mining and high rise construction. In the United States, it has been estimated that one out of every five patients admitted to a typical research hospital acquires an iatrogenic illness, with half of these episodes resulting from complications of drug therapy and a surprising 10 per cent from diagnostic procedures. Before you let it pass as another piece of statistics, let me give you the English meaning of the impressive term I used just now—*iatrogenic* illness. In Greek *iatros* means physician and *genesis* means origin and *iatrogenic* illnesses are the illnesses generated by the medical care process itself.

Let us go simple. Let us look at basic things. The origins of disease are generally found in several causative factors that result in ill health. Morever, their effects differ profoundly from person to person, since they depend on the individual's emotional reactions to stressful situations and on the social environment in which these situations occur. The common cold is a good example. It can develop only if a person is exposed to one of several viruses, but not everybody exposed to these viruses is afflicted. Exposure results in illness only when the individual is in a receptive state, and this depends on weather conditions, fatigue, stress and a host of other circumstances that influence the person's resistance to infection. To understand why a particular person develops a cold, many of these factors have to be assessed and weighed against one another. Only then will the 'puzzle of the common cold' be solved.

This situation has its counterpart in almost all illnesses, most of them far more serious than the common cold. An extreme case, in both complexity and severity, is cancer. In 80's huge amounts of money were poured in the West into cancer research with the aim of identifying a virus that causes the disease. When this line of research remained fruitless, attention shifted to environmental causes, which again proved futile. Though certain carcinogenic environmental substances like asbestos causing lung cancer were found out, the incidence of lung cancer did not answer why only one in a thousand exposed develops the disease. It is very clear to me that any noxious influence from the environment involves the organism as a whole, including the psychological state and the social and cultural conditioning of the person. In the process of reducing illness to disease, the attention of physicians has moved away from the patient as a whole person. Whereas illness is a condition of the total human being, disease is a condition of a particular part of the body, and rather than treating patients who are ill, doctors have concentrated on treating their diseases. Clinical experience has shown repeatedly that one can be ill without having a disease. Half of all visits to doctor are for complaints that cannot be associated with any physiological disorder.

The mental fixation of doctors with disease has led to treatment to fix biological abnormalities. But this does not necessarily restore the patient to health, even if the treatment is successful. For example, therapy may result in the complete regression of a tumour without making the patient well. Emotional problems may continue to affect the patient's health and, if not dealt with, may produce a recurrence of the malignancy. On the other hand, it may happen that a patient has no demonstrable disease but nevertheless feels quite sick. Every doctor sees such patients helplessly.

Each disease in a wider sense can be seen as the symptom of an underlying illness whose origins are rarely investigated. To do so would require seeing ill health within the broad context of the human condition, recognising that any illness or behavioural disorder of a particular individual can be understood only in relation to the whole network of interactions in which that person is embedded. Where is this kind of effort? Who has the time? A patient in New York sent me a letter a week before he died:

If I had my life to live over, I'd try
To make more mistakes next time.
I would relax. I would limber up, I would be crazier.
I would have more actual troubles
And fewer imaginary ones.
And I would ride more merry-go-rounds, and
Catch more gold rings, and greet more people, and
Pick more flowers, and dance more often.
If I had it to do all over again.
But you see, I don't.

Perhaps the most striking example of the emphasis on symptoms rather than underlying causes is the drug approach of contemporary medicine. It has its roots in the erroneous view that bacteria are the primary causes of disease, rather than symptomatic manifestations of underlying physiological disorder. In suppressing or alleviating the symptoms by destroying bacteria instead of looking for the causal roots of the disorder caused irreparable damage to the organisms of millions of patients. Many were rendered resistant to life-saving antibiotics through their use for common cold and other trivial inconveniences while many others had their immunological systems impaired. It is so well known that many types of bacteria and viruses associated with disease are commonly present in the tissues of healthy individuals without causing any harm. Only under special circumstances that lower the general resistance of the host do they produce pathological symptoms. A majority of children from affluent families raised under totally germ-free environments in air-conditioned homes grow into asthmatic adults.

Out of the huge population of bacteria on the earth only a small number is capable of generating diseases in human organisms, and these are usually destroyed in due course by the organism's immune mechanisms. The man who catches a meningococcus is in considerable less danger of life, even without taking antibiotics than meningococci unlucky enough to catch a man. The point is that the development of infectious diseases depends as much on the response of the host as on the specific characteristics of the bacteria. There seem to be very few infectious diseases in which the bacteria cause actual direct damage to the cells or tissues of the host organism. There are some, but in most cases the damage is caused by an overreaction of the organism, a kind of panic in which a number of powerful, unrelated defence mechanisms are all turned on at once. Infectious diseases, then, arise most of the time from lack of co-ordination within the organism, rather than from injury caused by invading bacteria.

Given these facts, it would seem extremely useful, and as intellectually challenging, to study the complex interactions of mind, body and environment that affect resistance to bacteria. The practice of *pranyaam* and meditation to enhance mind-body co-ordination stands to be integrated into medical practice without any doubt of their usefulness whatsoever.

Antibiotics, of course, are not the only type of drugs used in modern medicine. Drugs have become the key to all medical therapy. They are used to regulate a wide variety of physiological functions through their effects on nerves, muscles and other tissues, as well as on the blood and other bodily fluids. Drugs can improve the functioning of the heart and correct irregularities; they can raise or lower blood pressure, prevent blood clotting or control excessive bleeding, induce muscle relaxation, alter the secretion of various glands and regulate a number of digestive processes. By acting on the central nervous system, they can alleviate or temporarily eliminate pain, relieve tension and anxiety, induce sleep or increase alertness. Drugs can affect a wide range of regulatory functions, from visual accommodation of the eye to the destruction of cancer cells. Many of these functions involve subtle biochemical processes that are barely understood, if not completely mysterious.

The extensive development of synthetic drugs in modern medicine has allowed physicians to save innumerable lives and alleviate much suffering and discomfort, but, unfortunately, it has also led to the well-known overuse and misuse of drugs, both by doctors through prescription and by individuals through self-medication. Adverse drug reactions and immunity against life saving antibiotics because of their use in insufficient quantities or during viral infections have already become a public health problem of alarming proportions, at least in cities, producing *paid* pain and discomfort for millions. Some of these effects are inevitable, and many of them are clearly the fault of patients, but many others are the result of careless and inappropriate prescriptions by doctors who follow pharmaceutical companies more than their pharmacological books. It has been argued that high-quality medicine can be practised without the use of any of the twenty most prescribed drugs. The World Health Organisation's list of essential drugs does not include even 100 drugs.

Many in the pharmaceutical industry scorn at *Ayurvedic* drugs and talk about quantification of active ingredients. While standardisation of herbal drugs is absolutely essential, they can't be treated as allopathic drugs. In fact some of the most effective allopathic drugs including digitalis, penicillin, and morphine—

come from plants and many of them have been used as medicines throughout the ages. But there is a crucial difference between the use of herbal medicine and chemical drugs. The drugs prepared in modern pharmaceutical laboratories are purified and highly concentrated samples of substances that occur naturally in plants. Though these purified products act very fast in any particular aspect, they turn out to be overall more hazardous than the original unpurified remedies. Though the crude extract from the plant acts slowly, it ensures that the body's reaction does not go too far and cause unwanted side-effects. Crude extracts of herbal mixtures also have very special antibacterial properties. They do not destroy the bacteria but prevent them from multiplying, so that mutations cannot occur and strains of bacteria resistant to medication are unlikely to develop. Furthermore, the dosage of herbal medicines is much less problematic than that of chemical drugs. Herbal mixtures that have been tried out empirically for thousands of years need not be quantified precisely because of their in-built moderating effects. Instead of suffering the side-effects of unwarranted chemicals we need to validate our heritage knowledge of herbal medicine.

Although physicians have considerable power to influence the healthcare system, they have become conditioned by it. Since their training is heavily oriented towards hospital care, they feel more comfortable in doubtful cases when their patients are in hospitals, and since they receive very little reliable information about drugs from non-commercial sources, they tend to be unduly influenced by the pharmaceutical industry. However, the essential aspects of contemporary healthcare are determined by the nature of medical education. The emphasis on hard technology, the over-reliance on drugs and the practice of centralised, highly specialised medical care, all originate in medical schools and academic medical centres. A generation ago more than half of all physicians were general practitioners. Now over 75 per cent call themselves as specialists. Worst still, general practitioners are seen as second-rate doctors by people. The fact, however, is that general practitioners not only require much broader scientific knowledge and technical skills than specialists, but also wisdom, compassion and patience. They need better ability to provide human comfort and reassurance, sensitivity to the patient's emotional problems and therapeutic skills in the management of psychological aspects of illness. The specialist-producing medical colleges of today appear like families where mother is gone and only the hard father remained at home. Any attempt towards change has to begin by changing medical education.

The purpose of our academic centres should not only be training but also research. Although epidemiological, social, and environmental research would often be much more useful and efficient for improving human health than the strict cause-and-effect kind of investigations, projects of this kind are little encouraged and poorly financed. The reason for this resistance is definitely the commercialisation of medical profession fuelled by various groups in the health industry. We really don't know how many Indians are hypertensive and what the etiological patterns of high blood pressure are. We have cardiologists who promote alcohol as a benefactor of the cardiovascular system. We have oncologists who smoke and chew tobacco.

Although there is widespread dissatisfaction with medicine and doctors among the general public, most people are not aware that one of the main reasons for the current state of affairs is the narrow conceptual basis of medicine, aped from the West ignoring age-old indigenous healing systems. Indigenous systems are looked down and considered cheap. Most patients do not understand its intricacies very well, but they have been conditioned to believe that the allopathic doctor alone knows what made them sick and that technological intervention is the only thing that will get them well.

This public attitude makes it very difficult for a progressive physician to change the patterns of current healthcare. I know several physicians who try to relate the illness to the patients' living habits but find again and again that patients are not satisfied with that approach. They want something else, and often they will not be content until they leave the doctor's cabin with a prescription in their hands. Many physicians make great efforts to change people's attitudes towards health, so that they will not insist on having an antibiotic prescribed for a cold, but the power of patient's belief system often makes these efforts ineffective. As one general practitioner tells me, "You have a mother with a child who is running a fever, and who says, Give him an antibiotic injection, and then you say, Injection is not required, and then she says, What kind of a doctor are you? If you don't want to do it I shall go to someone else. To run my business I give saline," the doctor said. In India you can buy antibiotics freely without any prescription. No wonder that Indian population has nearly become resistant to Amoxyllin!

Where do we go from here? I have attempted to explain that the development of illness involves the continual interplay between physical and mental processes that reinforce one another through a complex network of feedback loops. Disease patterns at any stage appear as manifestations of underlying psychosomatic processes that should be dealt with in the course of therapy. This dynamic view of illness specifically acknowledges the organism's innate tendency to heal itself—to re-establish itself in a balanced state—which may include stages of crisis and major life transitions. Periods of ill health involving minor symptoms are normal and natural stages representing the organism's means of restoring balance by interrupting one's usual activities and forcing a change of pace. As a consequence, the symptoms associated with these minor illnesses usually disappear after a few days, whether or not any treatment is received. More serious illnesses require greater efforts of regaining one's balance, generally including the help of a doctor, and the outcome depends crucially on the patient's mental attitudes and expectations. Severe illnesses, finally, will require a therapeutic approach dealing not only with the physical and psychological aspects of the disorder, but also with the changes in the patient's lifestyle and worldview as an integral part of the healing process.

These views of health and illness imply a number of guidelines for healthcare and make it possible to sketch out the basic framework for a new integrative approach. Healthcare will consist of restoring and maintaining the dynamic balance of individuals, families and other social groups. It will mean people taking care of their own health individually and as a society, and with the help of doctors. This kind of healthcare cannot just be 'provided' or 'delivered'—it has to be practised. Furthermore, it will be important to consider the interdependence of our individual health and that of the social and ecological systems in which we are embedded. There is no point in pushing the stress around—from individual to family to another family to community and back to other families, or to other individuals or from society to ecosystem whence it rebounds virulently. Look at riots, violent crimes and road accidents. Look at the plague in Surat. Look at Streptopylosis in Mumbai slums. Healthcare at all levels will consist of balancing and resolving the stressful situations by individual and social actions.

A future system of healthcare will consist, first and foremost, of a comprehensive, effective and well-integrated system of preventive care. Health maintenance will be partly an individual matter and partly a collective matter, and most of the time the two will be collectively interrelated. Individual health care is based on the recognition that their behaviour, their food and the nature of their environment determine the health of human beings. As individuals we have the power and the responsibility to keep our organism in balance by observing a number of simple rules of behaviour relating to sleep, food, exercise and drugs. The role of doctors and health professionals will be merely to assist us in doing so. I will be delighted to spend the rest of my years in mobilising grass-root movements to promote healthy living habits—whole foods, physical exercise, natural births, relaxation and meditation techniques, television-free leisure and emphasising personal responsibility for health.

Everyone wants to live a life that is free of illness. Any sickness triggers the primal fear of death in us. To most people, however, death remains a hidden secret. We are irresistibly attracted towards the very anxieties we find most terrifying. Every attendant by the side of a mortally stricken loved one brushes with the danger of death in a manner that is more emotional than any other experience one can ever encounter in life. Very few of us, including those in the medical profession, seem psychologically able to cope with the thought of our own state of death. The idea of permanent unconsciousness is too scary to even think of.

I am more concerned with human life than anything else in the whole cosmos; to me how a man lives is more fascinating than how a star dies. If there is a God, He is present as much in the creation of each of us as He was at the creation of the earth. The human condition is the mystery that engages my fascination, not society, country, humanity, and so on. To me, man is God, the centre of everything. Those who accomplish the most—measured in money, intelligence, skills, happiness, or love—are the ones who make the most of their genetic inheritance. Even identical twins that share exactly the same genes turn out differently. Whether we reach our potential depends on many factors, but we are born as unique individuals with our own distinguished characteristics and capabilities. There is also an inherent flaw built in each of us that has the potential of growing into a serious malady at any point of our life. Whether it turns into a disease or how much or how far is all unique.

We are a mythological nation. In our form of existence, myths overtake hard realities. I have, therefore, decided to take on to the myth of death as a central theme of this book and attempted to allay the fears that are built around this dreaded phenomenon. Other than accidental deaths, all deaths are a culmination of long drawn processes that remain with us in different forms and stages over long periods of time. Death is not an act, a moment, it's a process. Not death but the disease is the real enemy. The God, in fact, lives within us in the form of immortal genes.

Setting aside big words and complex explanations of the semantics that go along, it can be accurately said that death comes through one of five simple universal processes: the stoppage of blood circulation, the inadequate transport of oxygen to the tissues, the flickering out of brain function, the failure of organs and the destruction of vital centres. If we understand that these are paving stones which are trod by everyone, big or small, rich or poor, to his or her exit, a familiarity with them will certainly make the walk less stressed and more purposeful. If the process of death becomes just a bit more familiar, life will be less frightening. More awareness about death as an integral and inseparable part of life will allow one to take sickness in a manner that is less scary. Patients will be able to seek decisions that must be made with a mind that is less charged with half-knowledge, anxiety and unjustified expectations. It is my thesis that we are greater than the sum of our biological parts. We have a power in us to be still better than what we are at the moment. Even in adverse times, the choice lies to a significant degree in our own hands.

I have played a small part in the creation of the first truly super speciality hospital in this part of the country. Some generous friends even give me the credit of establishing modern radiology in the country. Paradoxically, I don't find myself at ease in today's high technology-based clinical settings. Somewhere there is confusion, an unsure feeling about whether it is all required. Have we not, as a society, created super speciality hospitals, intensive care units and emergency rooms, as specialised hiding places from death? There is a big humbug going around in the name of healthcare. Scientists, bureaucrats, journalists and wise men write often about death but have rarely seen it. Physicians and nurses, who see it often, rarely write about it. Most people, outside the medical profession, see death once or twice in a lifetime in situations where they are too entangled in its emotional significance to retain objective memories. As not many people die at home any more, very few of us actually witness death. The final approach to mortality of those who we love and with whom have been closest with in life is concealed in hospitals. An entire mythology has so grown up around the process of dying that the central issue of living healthy life is almost forgotten.

I have lived with the awareness of death's imminence for more than half a century, and saw several thousand doors people take for their exits. I am living my eighth decade. There is no way to foretell whether this is to be my last decade or whether there will be more. I maintain good health but beyond absence of a disease, good health is a guarantee of nothing. The only certainty that I have about my life, and by implication my death, is another of those wishes we all have in common; I want to exit without suffering. There are those who wish to die quickly, perhaps with instantaneous suddenness, perhaps in sleep; there are those who wish to go after a brief, anguish-free illness, just long enough for every one who loves them to be by their side. I think I belong to the earlier category. I believe in dying before death comes. The *world in me* must die before *I in it* die so that I can look back quietly and dissolve into divinity:

There is a flame within me that has stood
Unmoved, untroubled through a mist of years,
Knowing nor love nor laughter hope or fears,
Nor foolish throb of ill, nor wine of good,
I feel no shadow of the winds that brood.
I hear no whisper of a tide that veers,
I weave no thought of passion, nor of tears.

What I hope, unfortunately, is not what I expect. I have seen too many of deaths to ignore the overwhelming odds against it. Like most people, I will probably suffer with physical as well as emotional distress that accompanies many mortal illnesses. Like many of my patients, I too may compound the pained uncertainty of my last months by the further agony of indecision. It is a very difficult job to decide for a doctor whether to continue with a treatment or to give in. It is even more difficult for a patient to decide whether to be treated for the possibility of more time or to call it a day and a life. As Ramana Maharishi said,

Mountain of medicine!
Why hesitate to give the
Medicine ending confusion
Arunachala!

I have no fear of the future because I am completely convinced that the situations I have been thrust in are providential. I am doing God's work. I am walking in the centre of His will. He is leading me. I am following Him. He is guiding me. I am making His chosen decisions. He relieves me of responsibility when it is beyond me, and He knows when and where that is. Faith in God and innate goodness provide the perfect pathway from here to eternity.

□□□